The Key

to upgrading
your life

The Key

to upgrading your life

Nik and Eva Speakman

First published in 2017

Copyright © The Speakmans 2017

The moral right of Nik and Eva Speakman to be identified as the
author of this work has been asserted in accordance with the Copyright,
Designs and Patents Act 1988.

ISBN 978-1-911195-68-9

Also available as an ebook
ISBN 978-1-911195-67-2

Typeset by Jill Sawyer Phypers
Cover design by Alice Moore
Printed and bound by Clays Ltd, St Ives plc.

CONTENTS

Our thanks to everyone who has supported and believed in us, even before we proved publicly that the perceived impossible is possible.

Your support, belief, loyalty and friendship fuel our determination to share our message of hope and healing, regardless of people's past, pessimistic diagnosis or unjustified labels.

INTRODUCTION

We know that deep inside, everyone knows the person they would love to be, the life they would love to live, and yet there appear to be invisible barriers preventing them from living that life. We removed our invisible barriers with the tools we will now share with you so that you are able to remove yours too, and like us, live the life you deserve.

So how are we going to do that? Well, Albert Einstein said, 'Simplicity is genius,' and we totally agree with his statement. As a result we're not going to overcomplicate this book. We intend to keep it simple, effective and, most of all, life-changing. You won't have to read through pages of waffle in order to get to the point where you discover how you can make changes in your life.

In the same way that life should be simple, we also want to make addressing and changing negative behavioural patterns that way too. We really don't want you to have to do any more work than is absolutely necessary. We want this amazing process of change to be as straightforward as possible so you can get on with the important job of making yourself happier, feeling more fulfilled and allowing your life to flow more easily. Let's not lose sight here of the fact that, while we are keeping the information as simple as possible, there is work involved on your part. Once you have this information, the baton is passed over to you and you have to run with it, by practising and practising until your life is where you want it. Just the way that we did. You see, we always lead by example, so we're not teaching you anything that we haven't tried ourselves. We began practising all the keys outlined in this book as soon as we created them back in 1993, and since then they have become a part of our everyday lives. They are tried and tested. We know they work as they have brought immense happiness and fulfilment into not only our lives, but also those of the many people we have shared them with over the years in our private practice, our workshops and our events. That is why we are really excited for you right now, as when you begin to learn, practise and adapt the core schemas into your life, your life can become as fulfilling as ours.

UPGRADING YOUR LIFE!

We remember owning our first iPhones and being amazed how they saved us so much time by allowing us to access our emails on the go. Years on and our iPhones have now become mobile computers accommodating cameras, calculators, satellite navigation, maps, radios and a whole host of applications to cover literally anything you could want or need. When new smartphones hit the market, people scramble to be the first to own one, and when upgrades of operating systems are released we all upgrade to the newest and latest software so our phones are fully up to date and able to freely access new and exciting things. If only we had that same determination to upgrade our thought processes and beliefs so that we could update our behaviours in line with our life.

Just take a second to consider how many of your behaviours are no longer needed in your life as they are behaviours from older operating systems and ideas you had when you were younger. Well, just like your phone it's time to upgrade your operating systems, or schemas as they're known, to give you the best possible life.

So what is a schema? In medical terms, a schema is a cognitive thought process, and in psychology it is a framework that allows us to organize and interpret information. But, put more simply, schemas are learned or copied behaviours which then become an automatic reference for how we think, act and ultimately behave. In fact, the therapy that we developed over a period of twenty years is called Schema Conditioning Psychotherapy (not to be confused with Schema Therapy, which is a different type of therapy).

The eminent psychologist Jean Piaget defined a schema as, *'a cohesive, repeatable action sequence possessing component actions that are tightly interconnected and governed by a core meaning'*, or in simple terms, the basic building blocks of intelligent behaviour and a way of organising knowledge. You could also consider schemas as files within a filing cabinet in your brain, each file telling us exactly how to react when we receive incoming stimuli or information. So schemas are a 'learned reference' that allow us to be proficient in everything we do, from brushing our teeth to driving our car to how we communicate.

Take a moment to imagine that your brain is like a computer. What you learn creates a schema or reference (similar to software on a computer) which goes into a database within your brain. Your brain then stores this reference or schema, and will use it for specific acts, behaviours and reactions, whether good or bad, until such time as you condition or change that behavioural schema for a different highly emotional experience or by receiving new information or evidence.

For example, we all have schemas for a meal in a restaurant. The schema will be stored with a pattern that includes looking at the menu, choosing food, ordering food, eating and paying the bill. So whenever you are in a restaurant you will run this schema.

In essence, when we are born we are all a blank canvas – a 'tabula rasa'. Other than physical genetic differences, brain injury or a brain defect, everyone's brains have the same information and knowledge at birth. Therefore, what we learn through our individual life – from our parents, family and friends and our own individual life experiences and surroundings – completely dictates how we see ourselves and the world around us, and how we behave and react to any event or situation that we are faced with.

It's for this reason that we all see the world differently, and why you may see someone reacting about something in a manner that you may perceive as either irrational or brave, yet to them it's perfectly normal.

We are all born with a small number of schemas. These neonatal schemas are the cognitive structures underlying innate reflexes. For example, babies have a sucking reflex which is triggered by something touching a baby's lips. Similarly, when something touches a baby's hand the grasping reflex is elicited. The majority of schemas, however, are learned. They are learned as a result of copying the behaviour of our parents or people we're in close contact with, or through personal life experiences and our individual interpretation of those experiences.

We are born with only two 'fears': a fear of loud noises, and the fear of falling. This is why you will notice a baby jump if a door slams, or a toddler instinctively putting their arms out to catch themselves if they fall. However, these fears are primarily a protection mechanism and therefore are not linked to our 'fight, flight or freeze' mechanism unless a subsequent negative experience occurs. An example of this would be being involved in the aftermath of a bomb blast, or being pushed and falling on broken glass, etc.

It is only when we are in a heightened state of fear or anxiety, and our brain is provided with the evidence and justification that we need to be protected from something, that a phobia or irrational fear may develop. Again, this is entirely down to the individual as two people may experience the same traumatic experience, yet only one may develop a phobia as each interprets the same event differently. One may be rational and accept that this is an extreme event that is unlikely to ever happen again, whereas the other may unconsciously choose to believe they need to protect themselves against a similar situation in the future just in case the same experience occurs again, and this may create a phobia.

Although the majority of schemas are positive and hugely helpful in life, it is the negative or negatively associated schemas that cause the problems and, if not dealt with and conditioned, they could last a lifetime, causing debilitating and devastating effects on the quality of your life and those around you.

So you see, we are essentially the sum of all our schemas, and the bad ones can have a negative impact on how we act and feel.

Events can affect people very differently and can cause the creation of different schemas within people who experience the exact same situation. For example, Eva grew up in a house where alcohol was regularly abused, and therefore there are members of Eva's family who created schemas that cause them to believe that alcohol is a good way to unwind and deal with problems. Conversely Eva's schema is: 'I can see how destructive alcohol can be, so I would never drink often or to excess.'

The reason for the vast differences in people's beliefs, actions and behaviours is fundamentally a result of the fact that no matter what we observe, hear or experience, every minute of every day our minds are unconsciously asking the question, 'What does this mean to me?' The interpretation based upon our existing schemas or beliefs depends entirely on the individual, and therefore the resulting responses and behaviours are too.

You see, our brain interprets EVERYTHING based upon what is important to us, or how what we have experienced could or will affect us. Our mind then makes its own interpretation and adjusts it accordingly to create our individual thought patterns and schemas, and it is designed to stop us doing anything that may harm us, which actually means we are not designed to do anything really difficult, uncomfortable, dangerous or particularly scary. Our brains will protect us from all these things as our brain is trying to keep us alive.

In order to change – to be the best parent, the best spouse, the best you can possibly be in your job and in your life, to be able to achieve all those things you want to do – you are going to have to do things that are difficult, scary and uncertain, which creates this problem for all of us.

To be able, therefore, to change your life for the better you have to change your schemas, as it is schemas that drive your behaviours. In order to change your behaviours in a positive way, you have to challenge the schemas that are creating the unwanted behaviours and therefore having a negative effect on you.

We create so many inaccurate schemas as a child, based upon beliefs that we derive from parents and society. Those beliefs depend entirely upon what country we are from, what race, what gender, which religion and which social class. With this in mind, because our perception of everything in life didn't come from us in the first place, you can begin to realise that the 'truths/schemas' we believe, are simply the schemas that we have learned from others. It's easy, therefore, to comprehend that potentially over half of our schemas are based upon totally incorrect information, the opinions of others or our own incorrect interpretation as a child.

The reason we can confidently say so many schemas are based on incorrect interpretations is also due to the fact that numerous fundamental behavioural schemas that we each have were created as children, when we did not have the life skills or experience to create a truthful interpretation of that event. For example, as a child Eva believed that the school bully who called her fat and ugly was pure evil, and that she was entirely correct in her opinion that Eva was fat and ugly. Until meeting Nik, Eva believed that she was in fact fat and ugly, and her self-confidence was at rock bottom. Eva has completely conditioned this schema, and now understands that the school bully was the one who had self-esteem issues and therefore had to make herself feel better by inflating her own status, through destroying others, including Eva. There is no doubt that had Eva continued to believe the school bully, she would not be the person she is today. Was Eva fat and ugly? No! Was the school bully purposefully evil? No! Hence, this was a lie, and it's why you need to question why you do negative things and have negative thoughts, and then make changes, rather than just keep repeating the same old patterns and subsequent unwanted behaviours.

We would like you to consider that while you cannot control events around you, what you can control is your choice of what to focus on and what things mean, before subsequently choosing what to do. Ultimately these three things control our lives. Being in control of your life is what this book is all about. If you want to change your life, then YOU HAVE GOT TO change. If you want life to get better, then you have to get better, that's simply the only way it happens. We therefore want to help you change old negative truths, schemas, patterns, beliefs or behaviours in order for you to be the person you choose to be, without having to endure the internal conflict caused through wanting to behave a certain way and yet being driven by conflicting negative schemas from the past. Knowing that our brains are all more or less the same when we're born means you can be like pretty much any other person on the planet you choose to be.

For instance, if you have a couple of relationships that go wrong you could end up believing that all relationships are bad. You may choose to stay single for years and years, until you realise that, actually, it wasn't being in a relationship that was bad, it was being in a relationship with the wrong person. When that 'click' happens in your head and you stop blaming relationships and realise it is the incompatible partners that are to blame, you will feel ready to move on. You can then clearly see how wrong your old thought pattern (schema) was.

So why wait for years to turn your unhelpful thoughts around when you can do it right now? You can condition your old schema with new evidence in a split second, and that new positive schema can set you free.

Say, for instance, you don't trust people and you think they let you down all the time. As a result you don't allow anyone into your life and you end up feeling even angrier towards people because you're lonely. But the more people you let in, the bigger your world becomes.

We've let a lot of people into our lives over the years and, yes, some have let us down. But we've learned a lot from those people, so they've done us a big favour in the long run. This process of changing what could have been perceived as a negative into a positive is something that we hope to teach you in this book. This is an empowering positive schema or belief that will transform your life. Remember, there is always an element of risk involved in every aspect of life, but risks are worth taking. Risks without doubt create rewards, and as the saying goes, *'If you've done what you've always done, then you'll get what you always got.'* Risks are the opportunity for a new path and a new destiny, and after all, when you feel deep inside that your life should be better, doing nothing and expecting things to change is the biggest risk of all.

Remember, even if something does go wrong for whatever reason, it can never be classed as a failure because, brilliantly, there's no such thing unless you quit. No matter what you do, and no matter what the outcome, right or wrong, you have got a result! You've just *learned* something from that experience. You may have just learned how not to do something, but it's a result as you now know what not to do, so in that way it was a *success*. Every bit of feedback you get means more experience, and you could say that good judgement comes from experience, and experience most often comes from bad judgement! Ultimately, the more things we do and the more risks we take, the wiser we become.

If we decide to eat a strawberry and we've never eaten one before, we could discover we're allergic to it and get ill. But, on the other hand, we could discover that it's the best thing we've ever tasted. So many people are risk averse, but remember, no risk equals no reward.

Each of us is the centre of our own universe, and it's up to us how big, small, fun, fruitful or varied that universe is. You can either make it very bland by keeping yourself locked in and being insular, or you can open your world up to so many readily available and thoroughly exciting possibilities.

The simple fact is we're not born with negative schemas, we create them, and anything we have *created* we can condition and change. We just need to know how. That's what is at the core of this book. We will share with you the twelve key schemas you need to enable yourself to break those debilitating habits you've been carrying around with you for years, habits you no longer want or need in your life.

A BIT ABOUT US…

You may perhaps think, 'But how can you tell us the keys to success? How do you know what they are?' Well, we'd like to tell you a bit about ourselves so you understand where we're coming from and how working with these schemas has totally transformed our lives.

We met in 1991, and our relationship hasn't always been perfect, but we've always taken a step back and evaluated how it can be better. In doing so we've questioned everything and adapted our beliefs to make things *work*. As a result of that, we've created the twelve key schemas you're going to learn about (and then use!) in this book.

In order for you to fully understand how we got to where we are today, we feel that it's important that we tell you a bit about our background both as individuals and as a couple. People look at us now and say things like, 'You're so lucky,' but there is no such thing as luck. We create our life, and we create our own luck! By sharing our life with you, you will see that we've had our own obstacles to overcome, but we've managed to turn things around and have totally transformed our lives as a result. We've dissected all the negative beliefs we held and turned them into positives, and this book is all about showing how you can do the same.

EVA'S STORY

I was born into a Polish family, and when I started school aged four, I immediately felt very different. I was shy, and maybe because of the language barrier I fell behind academically, felt isolated from my classmates, and felt I didn't fit in.

Even though at home I didn't want for anything in terms of material possessions, my life was challenging. My dad liked a drink, and as a result there was a significant amount of turbulence, and I saw things that a little girl should never see. We had a lot of drunk people coming and going from the house, and understandably my mum would try to escape when she could. As a child, I wanted to protect her. I felt very isolated, yet at the same time I loved my dad, who when sober was a very kind and gentle man. The rages and aggression therefore caused a lot of confusion. From the outside, to others things looked great, but I was embarrassed about the fact that my mum and dad would argue, and that when Dad was drunk he'd blow up physically and verbally. I didn't want anyone to know about what happened behind our closed doors so I avoided having friends over, but when I did, I was petrified, uptight and full of anxiety until I knew that Dad had come home from work and was sober. If he was drunk, I'd laugh it off and pretend I'd never seen him drunk before and couldn't believe it!

My older sister and I had a rollercoaster relationship as it was either great or awful. There was a lot of sibling rivalry going on because she perceived me to be the 'favourite'. As a child I couldn't understand why she would be mean and argue with me. However, as an adult I now understand why she may have felt overlooked.

I had kidney failure when I was seven, and as a result ended up in hospital for weeks. There was a very real possibility I could die, and therefore I got lots of attention. I remember getting a 'Girl's World' (a doll's head to apply make-up on, which I had always wanted) and it wasn't even Christmas or my birthday! Although my sister genuinely loved me, and must have been worried that she'd lose her little sister, because she saw the whole situation through a child's eyes, she probably felt neglected and no doubt resentful towards me. Nowadays, we have our individual family distractions, and I do feel immense gratitude towards her as she lives close to and cares for our now ageing and disabled dad more, which is of course challenging.

As I can now understand her actions they don't hurt me anymore, but at that young age I had such low self-esteem I couldn't understand why she seemed to hate me so much. I thought there had to be a valid reason, and a part of that reason had to be that I was a bad person. I felt that I went out of my way to try to make her like me and please her, but it still it didn't mend our conflicts. I was so desperate for her approval that I would do anything she asked. It's such a little thing, but it made me feel weak. Thankfully, in hindsight I can see the reality of it all and I realise that her sense of anger wasn't about me, it was just directed towards me.

When I reached my early teens I was really grateful that my parents identified I was struggling academically, and they arranged for me to have a private tutor so I could keep up with the other pupils. It was then that I flourished at school. However, because I started to do really well in my classes, I then got bullied because the kids thought I was a swot. I was also a little plump as a teenager so I got called 'fat' and 'pregnant', and that affected me very badly. I had been brought up a Catholic, and as such had very strong views and was very opposed to underage sex and promiscuity, and therefore my world fell apart when someone said I was pregnant. As things do at that age, this hurtful and untrue gossip spread through school like wildfire, and I no longer wanted to go to the school I loved. I loved my teachers and their encouragement and praise for the standard of my work. I was terrified that I would be labelled, so despite enduring years of bullying at high school, when I never said a word to my mum, I decided to speak to her. Like me, my mum was furious, and for the first and only time she went to school to see my head teacher over a negative issue and to insist the issue was resolved, which it was.

After school I went to college, and met my first boyfriend, who was very sweet. However, that fell apart when he cheated on me, and I felt totally crushed. My self-esteem and confidence spiralled even lower, and this gave the schema I'd created at school that I was fat and ugly even more gravitas and was evidence that it must be true. I went on to become obsessed about my weight and, there-fore, weight loss. As my weight plummeted, as is often the case with anorexia my clothes became baggier to hide my skeletal frame. I then met my second boyfriend, who, as often happens, was a replica of my father. He was a big drinker and very violent, but because I'd seen so much of that behaviour at home, I assumed it was acceptable. I made excuses for the way he acted and rational-ised it. I blamed the drink and his friends, and justified how awful he was by telling myself that he loved me, while ignoring huge evidence to the contrary.

Our definition of behaviour is based upon what we see, in the same way you know an apple is an apple because you've been told and shown. My definition of love had been shaped because of what I had seen and been taught. I had witnessed someone close to me being hit, and then told they were loved seconds later. That then became what love meant to me, and why I deemed it to be acceptable to accept violence in the relationship.

At one point things got so bad that my boyfriend headbutted me and fractured my skull. I've never felt such excruciating pain in my life. I was in a nightclub, and I was so ashamed. I blamed myself, and felt people would judge me as I must have provoked the attack. I was so glad my cousin and best friend was there. She took me straight to hospital, and I just have a hazy memory of pain and begging them to please take it away. I was in such agony and felt such despair that I didn't know how I could come back from it. I had got myself into such a destructive situation and I was so incredibly unhappy. My self-esteem was on the floor and I knew I was losing the fight to want to carry on living. I didn't have the emotional skills to get through it. Or at least I didn't think so. But what I've learned in life is that you always have options, no matter how bad or dark things may seem. Looking back, although what happened was very traumatic, once I got even the smallest amount of strength back I knew I had to turn things around or I'd forever be in a similar situation.

That event and all the other negative things that were happening in my life at the time helped to teach me what I *didn't* want in life. They also made me start thinking about what I *did* want and how I could make my life better. I felt empowered by the fact I had made a decision to take action, and I accepted responsibility for everything that had happened to me. I realised that there would be only one person with me twenty-four hours a day, seven days a week for for the rest of my life, and that person was ME. As soon as I had this realisation, I started to move on and change the patterns that were marring my life.

NIK'S STORY

I have a similar story to Eva in that I was a very ill child. I had terrible eczema, and from an early age I was seeing doctor after doctor none of whom offered help, other than steroid creams. The most reassurance my parents were offered was that perhaps I would 'grow out of it'. I used to go to bed with several different creams on, and I'd be wrapped up in bandages like a mummy to stop me scratching at my body.

My parents devoted themselves to me, and my brother, who is two years older than me. Until I was born everything had been about him. He was the centre of my parents' universe until I came along. Apparently, a few weeks after bringing me home from hospital, my brother asked my parents to please take me back. However, as he was just two, that was entirely understandable, because when I arrived I began getting some of the attention that had been all his, and being a baby I wasn't even fun to play with. Looking back, I feel sorry for my brother, as not only did I rock his world and take some of the attention he'd had from my parents, but when I was about five I compounded the situation by developing severe asthma. One of my earliest memories is of our family holiday to Blackpool. On the day we arrived I had such a bad asthma attack that I had to spend the entire two weeks in hospital, initially in intensive care. Of course, my brother was too young to understand that I was sick, and as far as he was concerned I'd totally ruined his holiday. He didn't get to enjoy all the fun of the Pleasure Beach because my parents spent most of the time by my bedside.

Throughout my schooldays I was constantly on steroid tablets or injections and antibiotics due to my illnesses. My mum justly became over-protective of me and always used to say that she had to 'wrap me in cotton wool'. The slightest sniffle meant that she kept me home from school, resulting in my school attendance being only fifty-six percent. I didn't have many friends because I was ill so often, and I didn't have the time to develop friendships. My mum had seen me nearly die twice, so she was understandably very protective of me, and as a result my childhood felt restricted compared to others'.

The first turning point in my life came for me when I was thirteen and I was watching *The Russell Harty Show*. Arnold Schwarzenegger was a guest because he was promoting a film called *Pumping Iron*. From the moment I saw him he amazed me. 'How could someone become so fit and muscular?' I was this frail little boy who was immensely thin and was being bullied at school. On top of that a chest infection could be fatal, so Mum didn't really want me playing outside in cold weather. That one interview made me stop and think, 'Do I really have to put up with this? Is this how my life is going to be forever, or can I do something about it?'

That moment I transformed my way of thinking. I started reading about Arnie and he inspired me to change. We'll talk about his story in more detail later in the book, but to this day he remains my biggest role model.

Off the back of my newfound love and respect for Arnie I decided to start bodybuilding. My dad was also very much into keeping fit (or 'physical culture' as he used to call it), as he had previously been inspired by Charles Atlas. I began using his chest expanders and other equipment, and I dreamed of being fit and healthy for the first time in my life, as I now considered that, quite possibly, good health could be a choice.

I wasn't particularly knowledgeable about bodybuilding, but I knew that to build more muscle in my body I needed to eat more protein. It was not possible to consume the amount of protein required just from food, and therefore I looked at supplementing my protein intake with protein powders, which back then were high in dairy derivatives; furthermore it was common practice to mix them with milk too. Sadly, I wasn't aware of the damage that all the years of antibiotics and steroids had done to my body and particularly my bowel. Also, unbeknown to me at the time, drinking milk could have been deadly and was the worst thing I could have done. Having overcome my eczema and successfully managing my asthma, by the age of twenty I became very ill again.

I started to lose blood when I went to the toilet, which, being a typical guy, I initially ignored, hoping it would get better itself, until one day I collapsed and was admitted hospital. I felt so ill I honestly thought I was dying. I had ignored the fact my abdomen was swollen, my skin had gradually turned grey and I had no energy. I didn't even feel I had the energy to fight whatever was happening to me. I had a barium enema, and they diagnosed a chronic inflammatory bowel disease called ulcerative colitis, which affects the lining of the large intestine and rectum. Ulcers and abscesses develop, and these cause bloody stools, diarrhoea, abdominal pain and bleeding.

My body had become toxic and I was being poisoned by my waste via the open abscesses and ulcers. The consultant gastroenterologist said it was so bad that toxic megacolon had begun to set in, and therefore they would have to remove my bowel otherwise the poisoning would kill me or my colon would rupture within weeks.

A specialist came to my bedside and talked me through the proctocolectomy and ileostomy, followed by living with a colostomy bag. I was naturally horrified at the thought of having to have such a huge operation at such a young age, one that would make my life potentially so difficult moving forward. I was working in the banking industry at that time so I had the benefit of private medical insurance, but despite seeing the top consultants in the country I was told that there was no other option available to me as all the medication, steroids, steroid enemas and anti-inflammatories were just not working.

I was at the lowest point of my life and I remember lying in hospital thinking I'd had enough. I knew there had to be another way to get better, other than having such a major operation and a colostomy bag. People were discovering and learning new things every day and I knew that someone, somewhere would have an answer.

My dad always told me, 'There is always a way, and the answers to anything you need to know will be in the library,' so I decided to find a way to get better. I signed myself out of hospital, despite being told I could potentially die, and I went to the library and read up on everything I possibly could about the digestive system and bowels. I came to the conclusion that there is a lot of truth in the statement 'You are what you eat.' I wasn't born with my bowel problem, but it developed because my body had been abused as a side effect of all the prescription medication I had taken as a child.

I decided to cut out food for one week and have nothing but water to see what effect that would have, as I figured open ulcers and abscesses would not heal if waste was constantly passing over them. Gradually I started to feel a little better. I read that one of the least intrusive foods you can give your body is brown rice, and it is also a great complex carbohydrate, so I introduced a small amount six times a day into my diet.

My health literally began to transform. I then introduced other foods into my diet one at a time to see if I could tolerate them. This helped me categorise foods into foods that healed me, foods that gave me energy and foods that made me ill. The day I tried milk again I was cripplingly ill within an hour. The excruciating pain and bleeding resurfaced, and that was when I discovered that milk and dairy products had quite literally been killing me.

Within a year I had stopped all my anti-inflammatory medication and I became better.

While I was thrilled with my new discovery, I was also angry at the consultants who got it so wrong. So much so that I went back to see the hospital consultant to share my medical transformation with him and to ask him how he could have got it so wrong, potentially ruining my life. He had no real answers, and just kept saying that he wanted to 'save my life'. This changed my life as my anger became a massive realisation that he was right, however he only knew what he had been taught! Furthermore he was a surgeon and his job in the simplest of terms was to cut people open and remove the bad stuff, not to look for alternatives. So if the information is flawed, the actions and results will also be flawed. The medical journals aren't always right, and neither are the consultants. It's not because they're lying to us or don't care, it's because they totally believe and are genuinely trying to help you using the information they were given at medical school. However, one enormous lesson that I would like to share is that there's absolutely nothing to stop you challenging anything you're told. After all, it's just an opinion based upon learning. If the information or interpretation is wrong, then the learning will be too.

From that day forward I changed my belief system one hundred percent and decided to start listening to myself more. I also researched everything to look for different ideas, answers and viewpoints. I basically stopped letting other people dictate my life.

For so many people, life is what happens to them, not what they make happen. They're told what to do and think according to the rules, views and standards imposed by their employer, the TV, their parents or their partner. I'm not saying for a minute that you shouldn't listen to what doctors say, because of course they're trying to help you. But if you believe there is another way, then there probably is.

My dad was a massive role model to me growing up because his schema was that there was nothing that couldn't be fixed. I had now experienced and had full-on, categorical evidence of this with my chronic ulcerative colitis. He always worked hard and focused on what he wanted, and if things went wrong, he made them right, so he was an amazing person to learn from. He didn't moan, he didn't feel sorry for himself whatever happened to him, he just found a way to make things work.

During that period of time I changed from being someone who was ill and dying to someone who knew and believed that anything was possible, and I have been that way every day since.

NIK AND EVA: THE DAY WE MET

The day we met changed both of our lives forever, and for the better. Here's the story of how we found each other and what happened next.

Eva
When Nik and I met I was working in a bank, and because he was a financial advisor, I would visit his office to try and encourage him to use our banking facilities for his clients. Kind of like a sales rep,

I guess. When I first met him I thought he was overconfident and perhaps even a bit arrogant. But all that changed one day when my car got stolen from outside his office. I was only twenty-one, in a new job with a beautiful company car, and Nik was a complete knight in shining armour to me.

He was due to go to America in the early hours of the following morning, yet instead of going home and packing, he was busy looking after me and making sure that everything got sorted out. I was so grateful that I offered to take him out for dinner to say thank you. It was all meant completely innocently, but we instantly hit it off.

In view of what had happened to Nik with his health years earlier, he had already started questioning behaviours and results, which led him to learn about psychology, nutrition and self-development. He talked about it so passionately that it kick-started something in me too.

Nik used to read a new psychology book every week, and the first time we went on holiday together as a couple he gave me a self-development tape to listen to while I was sunbathing by the pool. I was a bit cynical, but it turned out to be fascinating. The guy on the tape confirmed how important it is to plan your life, something that I'd never considered before. When I finished listening, Nik asked me if I would be willing to plan my life with him if we stayed together.

From that day onwards we started writing down all of our goals. It was such a turning point for me, and also for us a couple.

Before then no one had ever asked me what I wanted in life. I knew what I *didn't* want, but I'd never considered what my future plans were. I had a good job and I was doing well for myself, but I was kind of plodding along hoping for the best. It never crossed my mind that I could decide everything that my future would hold.

I maintained a healthy scepticism, but two weeks later something incredible happened: one of the things I'd written down on my list came true. Then suddenly other things started to come true too. It was like magic, and I was hooked! I now had the knowledge that I could create my own path, and I realised that if I didn't plan my life, I would be working to someone else's plan. That knowledge was the first key to fulfilment, and it is still incredibly powerful.

Nik

When Eva and I met we realised that we both wanted our lives to have more depth and more meaning than either of us had ever experienced before. We had both had relationships that didn't work, and we didn't want to repeat those negative patterns. I'd had a big wake-up call, and as awful as it was, it taught me so much.

Prior to meeting Eva, I had been in a relationship for some years. However, we became incompatible as we were young when we met and as a result we grew in different directions. When the relationship ended, she and, shortly afterwards, her new husband, who I knew well as he had previously carried out work for me, denied me access to my two-year-old son. After numerous court appearances pursuing access, I was faced with one of the most difficult decisions of my life: I could continue with court action and potentially send the mother of my son to prison for flatly denying access; or, with the knowledge we just didn't see eye to eye any more, her new husband was a nice, kind and compassionate guy and she was still a good person and a very exceptional mother who just saw the world from a different perspective to me, I could walk away.

I was devastated at the time and I still feel incredibly sad about it. However, Eva and our children Olivia and Hunter are waiting in anticipation of the day my son gets in touch.

When Eva and I met, we decided that if we were going to enter into a relationship we were going to do it right and set ourselves up for the rest of our lives. While we could both have easily slipped into just another relationship and carried on that pattern forever, we documented the lessons we had learned and we were ready to change. People say to us, 'Well, it's alright for you because your relationship is great,' but that's because we found a way to make it like that. We made a decision and we both gave equal commitment to it.

Together we learned that we are all masters of our own destiny, but we give everybody else power over us, which is a mistake most people make.

However you feel about religion, it can be very misleading because it means that someone else is dictating your fate. I'm not saying that there's no God, and I don't want to offend anyone, but you have to consider that any God would want you to be happy. That's why they've given you the power to determine your own destiny. Once you say, 'I'm going to take this power back,' things begin to shift.

Up until she met me, Eva thought everything was in the lap of the gods, and she was floating along waiting for things to happen. But she discovered that she could decide what the rest of her life held and she acted upon that.

We're still 'normal', though, and over the years we've endured ups and downs, probably the most upsetting being Eva's dad getting in trouble with the law some fifteen years ago when he was very drunk. After fifty-six years of happy marriage my dad passed away, and then a few years later my mum did too. External events over which we have no control will always continue to happen, but it's how you choose to view them and deal with them that counts.

Since we developed our system, all of our dreams have been unlocked and come true.

We have an amazing home, two incredible children, we're both healthy and we're working to get our message that there is always a way to as many people via as many mediums as we can. We're changing lives in private practice, on TV, online via our YouTube channel and by hosting workshops around the world so we can reach out and help more and more people. It's everything we planned for, and it certainly hasn't happened by chance.

HOW WE CREATED THE
TWELVE KEY SCHEMAS

The twelve key schemas came to us during a series of conversations early on in our relationship. Eva was still reeling from her bad relationship, she was angry towards her sister and the school bully, and she felt resentful towards her dad due to his drinking. She was also angry with herself for having put up with so much, and felt so much shame and regret for things that had happened in the past.

Likewise, Nik was still upset from the breakdown of his relationship and the loss of his son, and he was still working hard trying not to feel like a victim due to his illnesses.

All of these thoughts and feelings were doing us no favours at all. Blame and regret are two of the worst, most pointless emotions you can inflict on yourself.

Through the process of getting to know each other we learned so much, and we then sat down and wrote a plan of our life together. It's as simple as that. You plan short-term things like going on

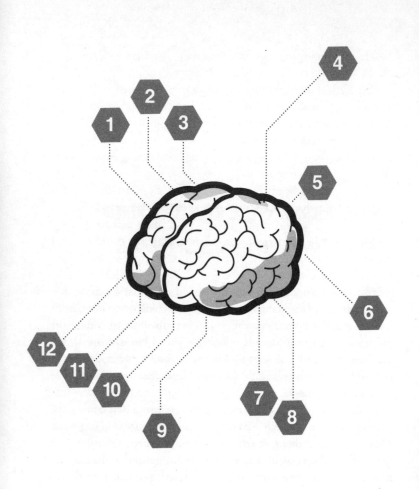

holiday the following year, but we decided to plan everything in the long term too.

We looked at everything, from where we wanted to live even to how *long* we wanted to live. We looked at things that may hold us back in an emotional sense, and worked out where we'd put up invisible barriers due to negative schemas we had created from our past experiences, and the best ways to break them down. Since then, nothing has stopped us.

A good example of this is the story of Eva and the London Marathon. Eva had always wanted to run the London Marathon, but when she vocalised it the kids at school laughed at her because not only was she overweight, she did everything she could to avoid going to sports lessons so she didn't have to wear tight-fitting clothes. Even as a grown woman, something was stopping her from applying. Ironically, it was nothing more than a lack of belief that she could do it.

At that point she was going to the gym regularly, had lost weight and was in the perfect position to apply, but without realising it she was actually protecting herself from failure. Unconsciously, she still believed those kids who laughed at her and told her she would never be able to finish (kids who had not been a part of her life since she left school), so she needed to challenge that old schema and condition it with a new one. Once she wrote down her goals – and a timeline for each – and planned how she was going to go about achieving them, it felt more real. She kept telling herself she would be successful, and even after not getting a place in the marathon for the first two years, she persisted, and when she finally received a place four years later she ran the London Marathon in a brilliant time.

If you know you want to do something but it's not happening, the first question you should ask yourself is always, 'What would I have to believe to make that happen?' The best answer is: 'Well for a start, anything is possible, so I'm sure to find a way.'

We have literally applied the blueprint that Eva used for the marathon to everything we've wanted to achieve. We've looked at what might hold us back or block us, and how we can shift those beliefs.

We were aware that there would be a transitional period to start with and that old behavioural patterns would try and keep us in the past – especially if you've had the same schemas for a long time, as behaviour and thought processes also become habitual. But we learned as we went along and lived by the rule that if someone in the world had done something that we wanted to do, then *anyone*, including us, could do it. Every time we came across an obstacle or something that wasn't working as we wanted it to, we questioned why and then readjusted our thinking and approach.

The most important thing we realised is that the first thing we needed to do was to take responsibility for everything we had done in our lives and to stop blaming other people. We also had to ask why we didn't believe we could do certain things, and what was holding us back. Once we had those two key schemas in place the other ten followed naturally.

Quite honestly, developing our key schemas did take a lot of work, and accepting and believing them took even more as getting to grips with them doesn't happen overnight for everyone. In fact, we found it hard to believe two of them at first, even though we knew that believing them would add greater depth to our life. But if you are willing to practise and use them as life-changing affirmations, they can work for you too. The outcome is so worth it because you're setting yourself up for the rest of your life.

We are not denying that in the future there may be more

schemas to add, but these twelve are a base to build from, and they're the basic ones everyone needs to know. You may even come up with some of your own while reading this book, and that's how it should be because it shows that you're taking control of your life and understanding what's holding you back all on your own.

HOW ADOPTING THE TWELVE KEY SCHEMAS CAN TRANSFORM YOUR WORLD FOR THE BETTER

A great example of someone totally changing their world through their beliefs is Susan Boyle. She grew up hoping, but never really believing, that she would be an internationally recognised singing star. Then one day she challenged and ultimately changed that schema when she went along to an audition for *Britain's Got Talent*. Due to her appearance, lack of confidence and lack of social skills, neither Susan, nor the public thought she would be a globally recognised successful singer, yet the moment she began to sing, her obvious talent shone through and the rest is history.

It may have taken her forty-eight years to get to that point, but look what happened when she did. Something clicked inside her for whatever reason and she suddenly felt good enough. She may not even know why, because sometimes you hit a threshold and change happens without you even realising it. Sometimes you don't need to know all the reasons behind a positive change, you just need to be grateful that it happened. Being open-minded and accepting change is one of the big keys to overcoming obstacles and belief systems that aren't serving you in your life.

There are so many people who don't think they can lose weight, and if they look deep down inside, they may be shocked to realise that they have an internal conflicting schema that in essence stops them losing weight to protect them. Maybe they're worried people won't like them as much if they're slim. Maybe they simply don't believe they're good enough to be slender. It can take one brief moment for someone to decide that they want to feel better about themselves, but until that schema is conditioned and change comes, they can go on losing and putting on the same couple of stone their entire lives in a never-ending pattern.

WHERE DO YOU COME IN?

In total, there are twelve key schemas that we're going to tell you about in this book. We're also going to give you compelling evidence that will make acceptance of these key schemas simple. This book is quite simply about YOU helping yourself and transforming your life from what it is right now to what you have always wanted it to be.

HERE ARE OUR TWELVE KEY SCHEMAS

1. There is no one reality
2. Disregard the doubters
3. Accept responsibility
4. Anything is possible
5. Failure only exists when you quit
6. It's never too late
7. Plan your life
8. You are what you eat
9. Save yourself before you save the world
10. There are no bad people in the world
11. You've got to give to receive
12. You become what you think about

We're sure that you may already agree with, or at least identify with, some of the schemas above. Over the next twelve chapters we're going to explain exactly what they mean, how they can benefit you and how you can start integrating them into your everyday life in a very easy way.

YOUR FIRST KEY – THERE IS NO ONE REALITY

As with all situations in life, it's important to look at things from more than one angle. When we see something, we instinctively apply our view of the world, our life skills and our knowledge to that situation and immediately make an assumption based on our personal experiences. Yet quite often we can be so wrong. For example, you might have personally experienced the situation of not having heard from a friend for a while, and you start wondering if you've upset them in any way. Then suddenly out of the blue your friend calls to say that their mobile broke down and they've been waiting for a replacement, so you've spent that time worrying unnecessarily.

We are big animal lovers and it upsets us that in China there's such massive poaching of wild animals because their bones are used for medicine. But even though we find that notion ridiculous, it's a part of their culture and they one hundred percent believe that those animals have healing powers. It may not be our reality, but it's theirs.

Think about it. If life was simply black and white and there was only one reality, we wouldn't need a judicial system. That's why we have a jury, so they can be impartial when both sides feel they're absolutely right in what they believe. People are prepared to spend thousands on lawyers' fees because they are so convinced that they are right. The amazing thing is that the opposing side thinks that too!

A further example to illustrate this is our son Hunter. He had the most horrendous eczema and we kept getting told that the best we could hope for was that he'd grow out of it. We didn't relent and never gave up because we knew there had to be an answer out there somewhere – after all, 'anything is possible'. After getting nowhere with several specialists and dermatologists within the NHS and privately, we then took him to people all over the world. Then, one day, someone told us about a South African dermatologist called Dr Richard Aron, who had created a successful method to manage eczema. He had blended three different creams, which are all available on the NHS, to create a certain formula. After two weeks of using it Hunter was eczema-free. We were so grateful that we invited Dr Aron to do radio and TV interviews with us, because he too wanted to get the word out about the cream to other doctors.

Most amazingly to us, the doctor didn't get a single phone call. He had used an antibacterial cream, a moisturiser and a steroid cream, and because the three products are made by different pharmaceutical providers, no one wanted to get involved.

That gave us further confirmation that companies ultimately don't seem to want cures, they want dependency. If they find a cure, they've lost their customers. Despite that, we knew that we would find an answer for Hunter, and the reality is that there is a cure.

But the pharmaceutical companies' reality is that there isn't, simply because they apparently don't want one.

We once worked with a doctor from Scotland who was involved in a pain control study and the effects of placebos. There were ten people who were in severe pain and being given morphine to control it. They were asked if they would like to participate in a study of a groundbreaking new type of morphine. They were all in severe pain and therefore all signed up. Every day a doctor visited them and injected them with this new wonder morphine. It was actually normal morphine but a slightly higher dose, and all reported they were pain-free. On day four, unbeknown to the participants, they were injected with a placebo that was quite simply a coloured saline that looked like morphine. That continued for an entire month, and by the end of the month nine of those who remained were pain-free. The tenth person, while considerably better, was still in pain. This experiment is testament to the absolute power of belief. Because the participants believed they were being injected with a new pain-killing wonder drug, the majority remained pain-free.

If a person has a crippling fear of spiders and they go to their doctor, they may be given anti-anxiety drugs that make them feel less anxious. However, if you take away that medication, the fear is still there. They are still scared. This is because the medication merely reduces the anxiety, which is the symptom. However, it does not eradicate the cause and therefore is simply just masking the problem.

These patients' reality was that the 'morphine' was making them better. They believed it, so they felt it. The reality was that it was nothing more than coloured salt water.

A lady once said to Eva, 'You're so lucky, you're naturally slim.' Eva had never realised people thought that about her because the reality is she was an overweight teenager and not slim by any means. She became slim when she started to take an interest in becoming healthier. These days she goes to the gym five times a week and eats healthily, and she's open about the fact that she works to stay in shape. Her reality is that she works very hard to stay slim, but the other lady's reality is that it's completely effortless and Eva was born that way.

It's also about putting things into perspective. We had a leak in our roof the other day, and instead of thinking, 'Oh my god! We've got a leak in our roof, we could have done without that,' we thought, 'We have a big roof, so we were sure to get a leak one day, no problem we can get it fixed.' The thing to do is to spin situations around and put a positive slant on them. It's not always easy to do when you're feeling angry about something, but once you feel calmer and you can take a step back, you can consider looking at things from a different perspective.

Shakespeare said, 'Nothing is good or bad, it's only thought that makes it so.' He is absolutely correct and the great thing about your thoughts is that you are 100 percent in control of them. You and you alone choose how you wish to interpret any situation. Thought becomes feelings, and feelings dictate action.

Every single time people come and see us about a bad relationship they're getting over, we ask them if they would rather have never gone through it. Nine times out of ten they say they would rather have gone through it and learned the lessons they did than have skipped it altogether – no matter how bad it was. But, of course, when you're in that bad relationship you can't see anything positive coming out of it.

Schemas mean we don't believe what we see, we see what we already believe.

Whether it's right or wrong, it's our individual belief. In 2011 the Irish traveller and former bare-knuckle boxer Patrick 'Paddy' Doherty went into the *Celebrity Big Brother* house. Having been labelled as one of 'Danny Dyer's Deadliest Men', it was expected that Paddy would be a troublemaker in the house. Remarkably, he came across as far from deadly. He was compassionate and supportive, and was praised by many of the housemates for the support he offered them when times were tough. He proved the critics totally wrong and went on to win the show. While we have never met Paddy, since the show we have met several people who were in the *Big Brother* house with him or who know him personally and they all said he is a really lovely guy. He is very happily married with children and being in *Big Brother* was the first time he had spent time away from his wife since they were married thirty-three years ago. You see, people chose to take his background and how he looks into account and judged him solely on that. This also goes back to the schema that says there are no bad people, just bad situations. Paddy is clearly a nice bloke, but since going on the show he's been slated in the press for having fights. That's not necessarily because he's a bad person, but because of situations he's found himself in. People he knew before he went on *Big Brother* have since tried to start fights with him, just to make a name for themselves. He comes from a world where fighting is the norm – it's what he grew up with – but that's not to say it's what he always has to do.

Now Paddy appears to have distanced himself from the people who were having a negative effect on him he's been in the press for the *right* reasons, like for making a great TV show. There may always be people from his past who will try and drag him back into violence, but he will always have the choice to walk away.

Over the years we've worked with numerous lottery winners, many of whom have experienced very mixed emotions. On the one hand, they're deliriously happy they've got all this money and perceived happiness, but the flip side is it becomes incredibly hard to know who you can trust, and more so to deal with the expectations of your friends or family, particularly if they're struggling financially. If someone wins £5 million and they give someone £50,000, some recipients may be thrilled, while others may think they're stingy and will slate them to friends and family. It's £50,000! That kind of thing can transform lives positively, or in other realities cause in-family fighting and leave the lottery winners feeling even more sad and confused than before they won the money. Our advice would go back to the key belief 'save yourself before you save the world'. There's only you that will be with you every minute of your life, for all your life, and therefore you owe yourself the respect of making yourself happy.

We went to visit a friend of ours in America a few years ago, and his uncle had just won several million on the New York lottery. He hadn't seen or spoken to his uncle since he was a small child, yet out of the blue he received a cheque for $20,000.

Our friend was over the moon and said it was an absolute gift from God because it meant that he could clear all of his credit cards. It had given him totally a new lease of life. We were thrilled for him.

A week later we met his sister and we said to her, 'What amazing news that your uncle has sent you $20,000.' She turned around and said, 'The stingy bastard. He's won all that money and all I get is a measly $20,000. He knows I'm a single parent and he's just won millions. How selfish can you get?'

It just shows how differently people can react to an identical situation. No matter how hard you try to do a nice thing, it will mean the world to some, and yet will never be enough for others.

If you won £10 million and kept going to your local pub every Friday night and buying all the drinks for everyone, some people would think you're amazingly generous, whereas others would think you're a self-important Mr Big Shot. You have to live your life the way you think is best for you and try not to think too hard about the consequences. People will always perceive things differently to you, and you can't keep everyone smiling all of the time. It's just the way the world works.

Remember this profound statement: '*I don't know the key to success, but I sure know the key to failure is trying to please everyone.*'

Today is the day that you need to get a happier, more positive attitude. Why? Well, give us one good reason why not, because we know you deserve it.

We spend so much time focusing on things that go wrong in our lives. We may achieve ten things in one day, but if one of them goes wrong, we choose to dwell on that and not the nine that went right.

We've spoken to so many celebrities who say that when they go on Twitter they can read a hundred lovely messages from people, but as soon as they read a negative one it can ruin their entire day. When they go to bed that night, that's the message they're thinking about, not all of the great things that have happened to them that day. It doesn't make any sense.

Society conditions us to concentrate on what goes wrong as opposed to what goes right, and it all begins when we start at school. We get little ticks and big crosses, often in red, on our work thus focusing our attention on what we did wrong. See? While this way of thinking starts at a very young age – it's never too late to change it.

Jo and Sam had been friends for over twenty years. Jo had always suffered from low self-esteem, and all the time they had been mates Jo had remembered a comment that Sam had made about 'none of their friendship group being anything special looks-wise'. As a teenager Jo had taken that to mean that Sam didn't think she was very attractive, and she'd let it eat away at her a little every time she thought about it.

Many years later, Jo decided to bring it up over a couple of glasses of wine and laughed as she remembered the time Sam effectively said their group were frankly rather plain. Sam was abso-lutely horrified. She couldn't even remember making the comment and admitted that she'd always felt like the ugly one in the group because everyone else was so pretty.

Jo had been carrying that throwaway comment around for all those years, when the reality was that Sam was the one who didn't feel good enough. Even though it was such a small thing, Jo's self-esteem got a huge boost that day because she was able to let it go.

Another good example is the story of a client whose mum had died when she was a little girl. From that moment on her world had become a nightmare. She admitted that it was chaos in her house when she was young and everyone was trying to get to bed. There were five children, and it used to be her mum who would look after everyone and ensure the bedtime procedure ran smoothly.

After her mum passed away, every night at 9pm her dad would turn off all the electricity in the house and send all the kids to bed without so much as a kiss or a 'Goodnight'. She had so much anger and resentment towards him because she felt like he didn't care about her or her siblings. She perceived his method as callous and loveless.

We said to her, 'Could it be that your dad worked all day, came in tired, fed you all, and when he asked you to go to bed, you all ran riot? Maybe the only way he could deal with getting you all to bed at once was by pulling the power so you had no choice. That may have been the hardest time of day for him as well, because he probably missed your mum more than ever then.'

The years of hatred and resentment melted away in front of our eyes. She admitted that she found it hard enough to deal with her own two children at bedtime, let alone all of the screaming kids he had to put up with. Her reality suddenly changed from resentment to compassion towards her father. She started to see things from his point of view and realised that he didn't turn off the electricity to be cruel. He just found everything too much to deal with.

Something similar happened with another of our clients, a lady called Amanda. She had a very high-powered job in the medical world but she was drinking so much that she was effectively an alcoholic. It had got to the point where she was drinking wine every day to suppress her anger and sadness. She saw getting drunk as the only way to deal with her emotions.

Amanda said the drinking had started slowly with a bottle of wine a day and had developed into three at the very least. The problem began when her dad died and she offered to build an annexe onto the side of her house for her mum to live in. She told us that she didn't understand why she did it (which is another schema – saving yourself before you save the world) because she absolutely hated her mother, but she felt obliged to take care of her. She told us that even seeing her or hearing her voice infuriated her so much that the only way she could deal with it was by getting drunk every night. She went on to explain how her dad had been a violent drinker when she was growing up, and whenever he got into one of his rages, her mum would go up to Amanda's room, close the door and put her heavy chest of drawers in front of it. Her actual words about her mother were: 'She brought trouble to my door.' She believed her mum was a bitch for bringing this madman to the door of her bedroom.

When we asked Amanda what she would do if a madman ever broke into her house, she replied, 'Protect my children.' 'So if your children were in bed, what would you do?' 'Run upstairs to the room and lock the door!' she said.

As soon as she said those words it all became clear. Her mum hadn't locked herself in her daughter's room with the intention of enticing her drunk, violent dad upstairs. She had done it simply to protect her.

As soon as Amanda could see that, the anger dissipated and she felt calm. As a result her relationship with her mum improved tenfold. She also reduced her drinking, eventually stopping altogether. Her reality was that her mum didn't care for her, but in fact she cared about her so much that her first instinct was always to protect her.

Exercise

Thinking the worst or being negative is a learned behaviour, and becomes habitual. It's time to break the habit!

The moment you have a negative thought or opinion, immediately add 'but…' Then find a positive spin, such as, 'It's not the way I would do it, BUT perhaps they haven't considered that,' or, 'It's not them, they're just products of their environment,' or, 'Perhaps in their reality they perceive…'

Practice makes perfect. Create new habits by adopting new behaviours. Initially this will take conscious effort, but eventually it will become an unconscious habit.

Affirmation

'Nothing is good or bad, it's only my thoughts that make it so. My new positive thoughts will therefore create a positive life for me.'

YOUR SECOND KEY – DISREGARD
THE DOUBTERS

I t was mid-June 2002, and we were having dinner with our close
friends of many years Matthew and Jean. During dinner we were
talking with real excitement about our therapy and the amazing
results that we were having. The conversation led to our thoughts for
the future, and without hesitating we shared how we felt that people
were suffering unnecessarily. As a result we realised we had to create
awareness of our therapy in order to help others by giving them hope
that they could be better. We figured the best way of doing that, and
to reach the biggest audience possible, would be to demonstrating
our therapy's effectiveness on television and in the media.

Our friends' demeanour altered, and in a very benevolent and
parental manner they said, 'Listen, we care about you and believe
in you, but you've got to be realistic and face facts: everyone would
like to get into the media and TV, but it's not easy, and to be
honest, it's highly unlikely.' Matthew then went on to say that as
a lawyer, he had represented a number of actors, and as a result he

knew at first-hand the difficulty of getting jobs in television and the media. Although his comments didn't feel great, what he said actually made sense to us in terms of why he had such a negative opinion about our chances. He was utilising his personal references (or schemas) from his actor clients to advise us.

Assuming our friend had a better grasp of the media world than ourselves (at the time we did not know anyone in TV or the media) we could have accepted we would be entirely out of our depth in an industry we didn't know and could have given up on our idea.

However, knowing that everyone is a product of their life experiences, beliefs and schemas (behavioural references), we knew that while the comments were made with the best of intentions they were based upon comments made by his actor clients. While we knew the task was not going to be easy, we were not actors who were looking to act or audition as his clients had.

Interestingly, our friends' comments were not made to shatter our dreams; on the contrary, it was to protect us from disappointment. However, had we listened, we would not have helped the hundreds of people that we have worked with through the medium of television or the thousands of clients we have seen privately over the years, as none of them would have known that we or our Schema Conditioning Psychotherapy even existed. Furthermore, our therapy would not now be in the process of being scientifically studied by universities in the Netherlands with a view to sharing it with the world.

Today, Matthew and Jean are still two of our dearest friends, and they're so incredibly proud of us. They often refer to that day, and also tell others about the day they told us to give up our mission to work in the media, and how we had proved them wrong. They are now two of our greatest supporters, and they always say that no matter what we say we are going to do and achieve that no

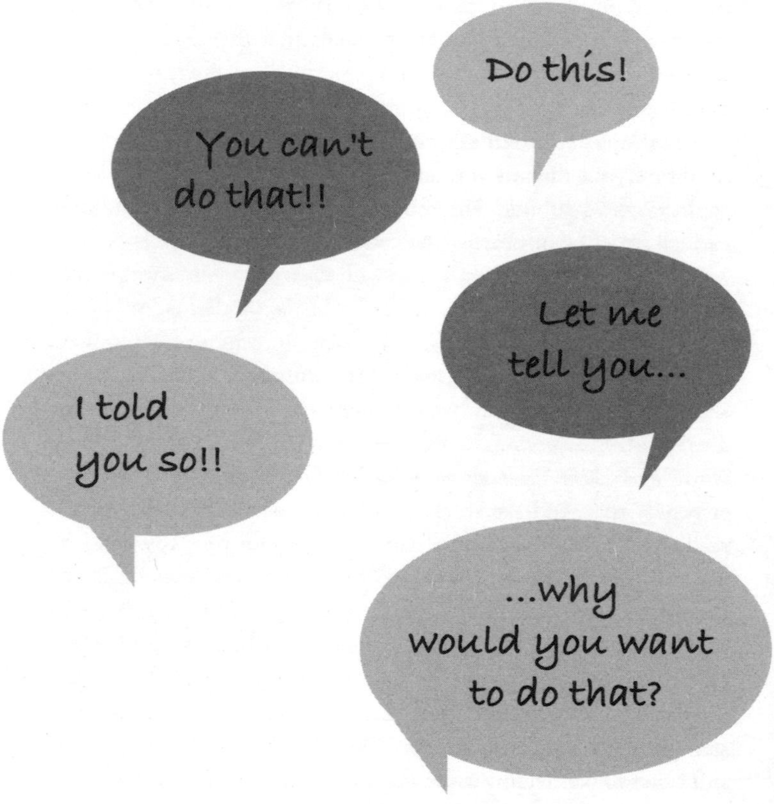
Do this!
You can't do that!!
Let me tell you...
I told you so!!
...why would you want to do that?

matter how crazy, improbable or off the scale it may sound, they know that we will achieve it.

It's so important therefore to disregard the doubters, as people can only give you an opinion based on their life experiences, knowledge and skills. This often means that they simply do not have the expertise to comment on your personal situation, dreams, desires and goals.

It is important to understand why people may cast a shadow of doubt on your dreams and ambitions, as it may not always be for the reasons you think. The motive behind anyone offering doubt can fall into one or more of the following five categories:

I wouldn't be able to do that:
An opinion based upon our own learning, experiences, intellect and ability. Naturally, an opinion can only be given based upon these references. For example, if your singing abilities are not too great and you were asked to sing karaoke, you most probably would not do it. Although you personally may never wish to doubt anyone, you could say to someone else that singing karaoke is a really bad idea as they can set themselves up for ridicule. When in actual fact they have an amazing voice and would really be setting themselves up for praise!

I might lose you:
Sometimes doubt can be given out of fear of loss. For example, you may dissuade your husband or wife to apply for a promotion at work due to you feeling insecure and worried that a new job could result in them spending less time with you and perhaps meeting new people. Or if you are really insecure, you may be fearful your partner may even end up having an affair.

From what I know:
Some people just like to appear as though they know everything. It gives them purpose and significance, so they comment to fulfil their needs as opposed to yours. For example, if you wanted to be an actor, instead of agreeing with you about the great lives actors may have, they will quote one person who regrets going into acting and then go on to tell you every way acting ruined their life.

I couldn't cope seeing someone else living the dreams I can't live:
Sadly, some people will cast a shadow on your dreams just because they find it hard to cope seeing other people living their dreams. Many people don't have the drive to take action, or they have low self-esteem or low confidence and so do not feel able to do anywhere near as much as you. This is hard for them as they become envious, and to protect themselves they try to sabotage your plans to help them feel better about themselves. Of course, this is not personal, and is often an instinctive response as opposed to one made out of malice.

I hate anyone doing well:
Some people quite literally just don't like to see others doing well. It's always beneficial to avoid these people at all costs.

You should always disregard the doubters and follow your dreams. After all, you really don't need anyone to approve your dreams. If someone else can't see your dreams, it's entirely because they are your dreams and not theirs. As we have said before, there is only you that will be with you every moment of every day and for the rest of your life, therefore other people's opinions should never dissuade you from fulfilling your goals. You really would be surprised at some of the incredible people who could so easily have quit had they listened to the doubters!

Having won an Oscar, six BAFTAs and more than fifty big-screen roles, Dame Judi Dench is one of the UK's most incredible and accomplished actors, yet at the start of her career one director told Judi, 'I'm sorry, you won't ever make a film because your face is wrongly arranged.' Had Judi listened, we would never have known her or had the pleasure of enjoying some of her remarkable movies.

Oprah Winfrey was fired from her job as a news anchor in the early 1980s for getting 'too emotionally invested' in the stories. Unbelievably, her boss at the time dismissed her as he said that she was 'unfit for TV news'. She proved her boss wrong on an epic scale as she went on to host a daytime show for twenty-five years, before launching her own TV channel. Oprah is now considered one of the most influential women in the world and is believed to be worth over $3 billion.

Sylvester Stallone says early in his acting career he auditioned for *The Godfather* and he couldn't even get cast as an Italian extra. It was just for a party scene with three hundred guests. Stallone asked why he didn't even make it as an extra, to be told, 'Well you just don't fit in.' At that point in time, Stallone said he felt like God was telling him something. But instead of giving up, he decided to take control of his life and write his own screenplay. Three days later, he finished the script for *Rocky*. Despite receiving a $360,000 offer, Stallone refused to sell the story unless he starred in the movie. Fast-forward a few years and Stallone's movie was nominated for ten Oscars, winning three: Best Picture, Best Director and Best Film Editing. Forty years later, Stallone was still rocking Hollywood in the Oscar race, after being nominated for 'Best Supporting Actor' in *Creed*.

At the age of twenty-four, Harrison Ford was told by a studio boss, 'You're never going to make it in the business. Just forget about it.' Yet he is still acting after a long and successful career that has seen him star in so many blockbusters such as *Star Wars* and *Indiana Jones*, and he recently revived his role as Hans Solo in the 2015 film *Star Wars: The Force Awakens*. Even now, at the age of seventy-five, he has just played Rick Deckard in *Blade Runner 2049*, reviving his character in the 1982 cult film *Blade Runner*. With a fifth Indiana Jones movie planned for 2020, this movie icon has well and truly put those early doubters in their place.

In the 1950s, John Lennon's teacher wrote that he was 'Certainly on the road to failure.' Yet Lennon and his friends conquered the world as The Beatles, changing the face of popular music and impacting the entire world. John went on to release solo anthems and without doubt is a British music icon and legend.

The professor who revolutionised physics with his General Theory of Relativity was told at the age of sixteen, by the head of his Munich school in a damning report that 'He will never amount to anything.' Yet Albert Einstein enjoyed a career showered with honours, including a Nobel Prize. Einstein later remarked philosophically, 'Great spirits have always encountered violent opposition from mediocre minds.'

The above are just a few examples of so many great people who could easily have had their careers utterly extinguished had they listened to the doubters, but no other human being has the ability to know what you are capable of. With this in mind, we want you to live your life for you, and no matter what your dreams, please know with absolute and utter confidence that any doubters should be disregarded entirely.

While you are now aware of the importance of disregarding the doubters you may encounter in your future, what about the doubt-ers in your past who are having an effect on your life right now? Have you listened to any doubters in the past and had their limits define you? How many years ago was it that you allowed some-one to tell you what you could or couldn't do in your life or what you were or were not capable of? If most people look at how they are living their life today, it will be according to a set of schemas that they created in their youth based upon other people's doubts. When we were very young or in our youth we often accepted opin-ions about what to believe, what we were capable of and who we were as a person, and those schemas then became invisible barriers that control our lives today.

A great example of this was taught to Nik by his dad when he was little. Nik said, 'I remember the circus coming to town during the school holidays as it always used to set up in the park at the back of my house. My bedroom overlooked the park and during the day I could see the horses, camels and elephants tied with a rope around their necks to a small stake in the ground, and I wondered why the animals and particularly the huge elephant just didn't rip the stake up and escape. Surely he could do that with little or no effort? I knew he had the strength to rip down the whole circus if he wanted to. I asked my dad why he didn't escape. He told me, 'The elephant doesn't escape because he doesn't think he can, due to the fact that he has been conditioned that way. You see, they took him as a little baby elephant who didn't have much strength. They put what was then a big rope around his neck and attached it to what seemed to him to be a huge stake in the ground. The baby ele-phant then fought and fought to get loose from the stake, until one day he decided that he was not capable of pulling the stake out.' Had he been a human, just telling him about his limitations may have kept him attached to the stake. Once that schema was created he would give up trying, as he would believe that his efforts would be futile and therefore pointless. The elephant, just like a human, would carry on with the thought that this is how it is, this is who he is and therefore there is no point in ever trying again.

We would urge you to take time to look at your limiting schemas, and even if they may have been true in your past, ask yourself truthfully, are they now? Were those beliefs even your limitations? Were they based upon any evidence you had then? When you have done this and you have a list, ask yourself, what can I do right now to overcome these? If you are like that elephant, as soon as you realise those limitations are nothing but a memory from the past and no longer apply, then you can change the memory, or condition it with new evidence, and this new realisation you will set you free.

Exercise

Go through your mobile phone list and add an icon of a flexed bicep or smiley face to anyone who you perceive as someone who is positive and totally believes in you and supports you. If in future you want any advice on anything you want to achieve, be sure to call and speak with those people (your igniters) only.

Affirmation

'I am capable of achieving all my ambitions. No other human being has the ability to know what I am capable of, nor has the right to take any of my ambitions away.'

YOUR THIRD KEY – ACCEPT RESPONSIBILITY

You can go and see every counsellor in the world, talk to your friends for hours on end over endless cups of tea, read every self-help book available and travel the world looking for answers, but as the only person who will be with you twenty-four hours a day, seven days a week for the rest of your life is *you*. You are the only one with the true power to change the things in your life that make you unhappy.

It's very easy to put your energy out into the world and hope that someone else will heal you, but no one can be by your side every moment of every day for the rest of your life apart from *you*. Although you may doubt it (sometimes because other people are very good at telling us how we should feel), no one knows you better than you do.

Friends, family and relationships will come and go throughout your life, so the relationship you have with yourself should always remain the most important. It's not about being selfish – we want

to make that very clear. In fact, putting yourself first is actually about being kind to others, but more of that later. Self-preservation is about taking the best care of yourself that you possibly can, and the pay-off is remarkable, not just for you but for everyone you love too.

The moment you start to take full responsibility for your life is the moment when you can truly start shaping it to become how you want it to be. Until you do that you will always feel that your destiny is in the hands of others and you're giving others power over you. It's easy to become a part of someone else's goals instead of creating your own, and as a result it becomes incredibly easy to lose sight of what it was you wanted all along. 'If you do what you've always done, you'll get what you've always got' – only you can change that statement.

With regards to negative feelings, you can only be negative if you can justify to yourself and others that you are entitled to be angry or upset for some reason. That is why you will notice angry people are always justifying themselves and the reason for their negative feelings. So, if you accept responsibility, you cannot justify your negativity and therefore you cannot be angry.

Only if you continue to justify negative feelings will those feelings control you and your life. As soon as you stop, accept and move on the negative feelings will vanish and you will become a more positive and effective person. Justification always requires that you make something or someone else the source of your problem, which means you stay a victim and the other party will always be an oppressor. Accepting responsibility will set you free.

This may be particularly hard if you've grown up with controlling parents or been in a relationship where your partner wanted to rule over you. If that happened, you fall into a pattern of thinking that other people know what's best for you. But no one knows what's better for you than you do. Don't feel bad if so far you have been swept along on someone else's journey because it's something that happens to most of the population at one time or another. But now is the time for you to change that.

The biggest part of taking back your own power is to realise that you don't need to be a victim and blame other people for anything that happens to you. As soon as you do you're putting them in control of how you feel. If you can accept that you've made mistakes or learn from a situation, you can move on and release yourself to live your life.

Not letting go is an anchor keeping you in the past. You'll carry around all of that hurt in a rucksack, and it weighs heavily on you. More heavily than you probably even realise.

For example, imagine when you're born someone comes along and gives you a nice, clean, empty rucksack to carry around. As you go through life that rucksack gets filled with things that have gone wrong, guilty feelings and things that have hurt you. Unless you let them go you'll feel bogged down, frustrated and exhausted with carrying your heavy load. Think of the elderly people you see who walk along with their shoulders hunched and their heads hanging down because they're carrying the weight of a lifetime of troubles around with them. The sad thing is, they probably don't even realise.

You are the master of your own fate, so let go and no longer blame others for what is or what could have been. Blaming others is the worst emotion as it keeps us in the past and away from our future. Focusing on and moaning about things that happened in the past which cannot be changed only serves one purpose, and that is to keep you in the past.

By accepting responsibility you stop giving socially acceptable explanations to socially unacceptable acts.

Michael Jackson's doctor Conrad Murray, for example, will forever be walking around with a big cloud above his head and the weight of the world on his shoulders. Some people say that all he did was what Michael Jackson asked of him, which was to administer a lot of drugs to relieve Jackson's pain and help him to sleep. It's likely he was begged for help and had a huge amount of pressure put on him, but as a result of his actions Jackson died. The coroner stated he died from a combination of drugs in his body, the most significant being the anaesthetic Propofol. However, instead of holding his hands up and saying he'd made a mistake and totally regretted everything that had happened, Murray denied that he'd done anything wrong, essentially blaming others.

If he had been honest about what really went on from the beginning, it would have been clear that he was remorseful and he would have almost certainly received a lighter sentence. People may also have actually understood his reasons and sympathised about the enormous stress he must have been under. Instead everyone was angry that he tried to shy away from any responsibility and acted in quite an arrogant manner.

Bill Clinton initially denied having sexual relations with his intern Monica Lewinsky back in 1998, and there was a massive backlash against him. However, as soon as he was honest about what had happened between the two of them, he was able to start rebuilding his career. Some people even had newfound respect for him. If he had held his hands up from day one and admitted he'd made a mistake, he would have saved himself an enormous amount of trouble.

Hugh Grant is another great example. At the age of thirty-two he claimed to be on the brink of giving up his acting career when he was given the lead role in *Four Weddings and a Funeral*. In 1994 it became the highest-grossing British film to that date and made him an international star overnight. In June 1995 he was in Los Angeles shortly before promoting his first major studio film, *Nine Months*, when he was arrested for committing a lewd act in a public place. He was facing losing his career and his long-time girlfriend, and even a potential six-month prison sentence. He could have made so many excuses. However, he took responsibility and said, 'I did something completely insane. I have hurt people I love and embarrassed people I work with. For both things I am more sorry than I can say.' Grant pleaded 'no contest' and was given two years' probation and a fine. Shortly after, he appeared on *The Tonight Show* with Jay Leno in a much-watched interview, when Jay Leno asked him, 'What the hell were you thinking?' Grant answered, 'I think you know in life what's a good thing to do and what's a bad thing. I did a bad thing.' And there you have it. Grant was appreciated for his refreshing honesty, and his career, relationship and life stayed intact.

It's fine to make mistakes – we all do because we're all human – but the buck stops with you when it comes to being honest about them. Once you accept responsibility you realise that you have been the only problem you've ever had, but you are also the solution. You can now draw a line in the sand, move forward and start to raise your standards.

Exercise

Taking responsibility can be tough. However, without doubt it is a decision that will totally change your life. The start of taking responsibility is firstly making the decision that you will. You might know it on the inside, but you may find it difficult to vocalise the words out loud so as to accept responsibility and then move on.

These steps will help you to accept responsibility and so release that anchor which is holding you down:

Day 1 – say the words 'I am responsible for...' in your head
Day 2 – say the words alone and out loud
Day 3 – say the words to a close and dear friend
Day 4 – say the words to a family member

You will notice it gets easier each day as the weight is lifted from your shoulders, enabling you to move on.

Affirmation

'As I am fully responsible for my life, I am responsible for... It was my fault. It felt right at the time, but I have learned from it, and now it's over and I can move on. This is my life, these are my choices and everything in my life is now my responsibility.'

YOUR FOURTH KEY – ANYTHING
IS POSSIBLE

You only need to look at the Paralympics to know that the above statement is true. Some people lose a leg and they're in a wheelchair for the rest of their life, incredibly unhappy and bitter. Then you have other people in the same situation who live a full and happy life, and even go on to win gold medals. One of the most amazing things we saw at the Paralympics was a high jumper who only had one leg, but he didn't let it hold him back. It was literally breathtaking to watch him.

In the UK we're socially conditioned to talk about how bad the weather is or to mull over some awful story in the news. When you ask someone how they are and they quite often reply, 'Not so bad,' what they're actually saying is that they're not so good either, so pretty low actually. We're used to looking on the down side of life because it's comfortable on some level. If we don't say we're feeling great, we won't feel like we've let people down when we're not feeling good any more. So we keep things on an even keel of 'okay' or 'not bad' in preparation for when something rubbish happens so that we're prepared and ready for it. This would suggest we're constantly in a state of negative expectation!

When the Olympics and Paralympics were on in 2012, for the first time in years the country – and quite possibly the entire world – was talking about how amazing it was, and no one even mentioned it had rained during the events. For the whole of the summer of 2012 there was a feeling of positivity in the air and everyone felt that bit happier because they had something incredible to focus on. A unity appeared and suddenly there was a commonality between strangers, who were then able to chat like old friends. Imagine how many friends we could all have if we took the time to chat to a stranger on the bus or train and took time to find a topic we had in common to chat about.

However, as with anything else this really is possible! We learn by copying other people, so if there's something you're desperate to do, just look at how someone else did it. It's not about reinventing the wheel; it's about using successful people for inspiration.

If you've always dreamed of becoming a runner, even just for a local team, but you keep making excuses not to do it, just think of all those athletes with prosthetic limbs who didn't let the fact they didn't have two working legs hold them back. There is always a way. Believe in yourself and you will find that way.

Society dictates that we should never tell other people how great we are, because that would be big-headed, so no wonder we find it hard to tell *ourselves* how wonderful we are.

If you blow your own trumpet, you're seen as arrogant, but why not celebrate how fabulous you are? For some reason it's fine for someone else to say how clever and talented you are, but if you say it, people think you're egotistical. Well, consider the fact that

if you don't blow your own trumpet, then no one else is going to do it for you.

Likewise, if someone gives us a compliment, we think the right thing to do is play it down or, even worse, disagree. If you think about that, it is unacceptable on two levels: 1) You're almost telling that person they're lying and that you don't believe what they're saying. 2) If you keep saying negative things to yourself, you will start to believe them.

It doesn't mean you have to reply, 'I know, aren't I incredible?' But a simple 'thank you' goes a long way towards making the flatterer pleased they made the comment, and also towards making you believe that their compliment is true.

We believe that we're the world's leading, inspiring life-change therapists. We don't say that because we're arrogant, we say it because we've worked incredibly hard to create a groundbreaking therapy that works in a remarkably short space of time, and by being confident in our abilities we've helped to save many thousands of lives. If we believe in ourselves, other people will too and they will be confident that we can help them. That's half the battle already won.

If people put us down for saying we're brilliant at what we do, we really don't mind because the pay-off we receive is absolutely huge. We believe in ourselves, and that makes us happy. And we *deserve* to be happy. We *all* do. Everyone has a right to be happy, whether God-given or otherwise!

If something is possible somewhere in the world, it's also possible for you. You could liken success to making an amazing cake. Say for instance someone spent thirty years of their life perfecting a brilliant cake recipe and it worked perfectly every time they used it. Out of kindness they post it on the internet and everyone else in the world starts following the recipe and getting the same amazing results immediately. It's the same with life. If you want to do something, find someone who has already achieved it and look at how they made it work. If you follow their method, you will eventually obtain the same results. You may be faced with different challenges along the way and have to change course, but remember that failure only happens when you quit, as every action produces a result. If you don't get the result you wanted, then as long as you learn, you become wiser by now knowing what doesn't work so you can try something different.

There's an incredible lady called Jessica Cox who was born with no arms, yet she can do remarkable things like drive a car and put in contact lenses with her feet! She is currently the only person in the world with no arms who can fly a plane. Imagine how many people would have told her that was impossible. There are millions of people who would find the thought of flying a plane terrifying, let alone someone with that level of disability. She is living proof that anything is possible.

Richard Branson is another inspirational figure. He apparently had a really hard time at school and was labelled unintelligent because he suffered from undiagnosed dyslexia. But he started his Virgin business by using a phone box as his office and making people think he was a successful businessman. He has had no more breaks than anyone else and has got to where he is by sheer determination, belief and hard work. So, if your plan for the future is to become a multimillionaire entrepreneur, read as much as you can about Branson and get some tips. If you know how to look for them, there are secrets in any successful person's autobiography, and his is no exception.

Sylvester Stallone's story is also amazing. He was born a forceps baby and as a result his face was disfigured and his speech was slurred. When he grew up he decided that he wanted to be an actor, but he kept getting turned down for parts because they told him he couldn't talk properly. He got so low as a result of being rebuffed that he lost his house and his wife and was left with nothing but his dog for company.

He used to go to the library to stay warm and he read lots of Edgar Allen Poe books while he was there. They taught him to think in a different way because despite adversity, Poe became one of the most applauded writers of all time. Around the same time Stallone watched a Muhammad Ali fight, and the combination of the two things inspired him to write the script to a film he called *Rocky*.

Stallone pitched *Rocky* to every film company going, until he found one person who offered to buy it from him for a lot of money. But the deal came with conditions – Stallone wouldn't be able to play Rocky. So, despite a good deal being on the table, he turned it down and walked out. He refused to compromise because his dream was to break into the acting industry by playing Rocky himself.

Stallone continued to tour the script around, refusing to give up until he found someone who wanted to buy the script and would also let him play Rocky. It took some time, but he eventually found them. The deal wasn't considered great as it was based more on profit sharing as they felt taking Stallone on in the leading role could be a massive risk. However, as we all know, the film went on to be a massive success worldwide, and he even won an Oscar for the script. When he collected his award he read out some of the negative things that people had said about him. A lot of those people were sat in the audience that night, no doubt kicking themselves.

After *Rocky*, Stallone had some facial reconstruction surgery and went on to forge an incredible acting career. He went from being totally broke to being one of the most famous men in the world within a few years, simply because he refused to give up.

On a more personal level, despite knowing it would be incredibly hard to find him, Eva's mum never gave up on finding her father. Eva's grandma got pregnant during the Second World War, and when Eva's mum was two, her father, who was a Polish Jew, left to go to Australia. He promised he would send money back to her grandma so they could join him once he was settled. As far as Eva's mum knew, that money never came and they stayed in Germany until she was a teenager, and she was then taken to England as a 'displaced person'. By this time, Eva's grandma had remarried, and her mum adopted by a horrible, abusive stepfather. She grew up never knowing who her dad was. Eva's grandma never spoke about him at all, and it was only when she was on her deathbed that she gave Eva's mum his name.

Eva's mum sat on this information for years because she was afraid of what she might find if she went looking for him. She'd built him up in her mind and put him on a pedestal. She was so frightened she'd be let down if she found him because she'd created a schema from her stepfather that father figures were bad news, but also as she had dreamed many times of him coming to rescue her and being a hero, she was scared of what she would find, if at all!

One day something switched inside her and she decided it was now or never. She got in touch with the Red Cross and told them that all she had was his name and the fact that he lived in Australia. They tried for months and months to find him but came up with nothing.

At that point Eva's mum could have given up, but someone came up with the idea of her hiring a private detective, and she felt like she had nothing to lose. Within weeks the detective had found her dad living in Sydney. Soon afterwards he called Eva's mum and all of her questions were answered. It turned out he had also tried to find Eva's mum numerous times, but her mum had moved them to England and changed their surname. Eva's mum found out everything about her background, and it answered so many questions and ultimately changed her life.

So many people don't love their jobs; they view them just as a way of getting paid and being able to live. So knowing that anything is possible, if that is your situation right now, then you have to follow your dreams after hours. If you work nine to five, then after you come home, eat and take the dog for a walk you have to work on you and your brand, whatever that is.

Exercise

Read autobiographies and research information on the internet about people who have transformed their lives despite massive odds. Think of ways you can apply their recipe for success to your life.

Remind yourself of things you have achieved, and of when you have been determined but thought you couldn't do something… but YOU DID IT!

Affirmation

'Remember every little acorn has a strong oak tree within it. If it's possible in the world, then it's possible for me. I can, I will, I must succeed!'

YOUR FIFTH KEY – FAILURE ONLY
EXISTS WHEN YOU QUIT

Failure only exists when you quit may seem like a bold statement, but it's just about looking at things from another point of view.

Every time you attempt to do something you get a result, and that result gives you feedback. From that feedback you can decide if something works or not. If it doesn't, you can try something else. So many people come to us and say, 'I've tried everything.' If they had tried *everything*, they would have the answer. If we ask them to name ten things they've tried, they usually struggle to even name five because they've generally tried the same thing over and over again, even though deep down they know it doesn't work.

The best example for the fact that there's no such thing as failure is Thomas Edison. It took him over ten thousand attempts to invent the electric light bulb, but eventually he did it and he completely turned the world on its head. It was certainly worth all that effort and he must have been hugely frustrated at times, but as the process unfolded he knew he was learning a huge amount and was getting closer to his goal with every positive step he took. He wasn't frightened of failing because he knew by failing he was getting ever closer to his goal of success.

It's entirely possible to perceive yourself as a failure if not everyone in the world likes you, so please remember this statement: 'I don't know the key to success, but the key to failure is trying to please everybody.'

We live by that because we know that you're searching for the impossible if you're trying to be liked by everyone around you. If people think badly of us, we're the ones who are failing by letting them have any kind of negative effect on us.

The bottom line is, not everyone in life is going to like you, no matter how hard you try. So stop trying to please others. That doesn't mean stop trying to be a good person, but stop trying to keep everyone happy because ultimately you'll make yourself unhappy and then you won't be as well equipped to look after the people who truly matter and care about you.

Often if someone doesn't like you it's because you remind them of someone they have had a bad experience with. When you hear people saying, 'Don't look at me like that,' to a total stranger, the stranger often has no idea they were giving them any kind of look. But the appearance or facial expression of the stranger may remind them of someone who was once unkind to them and treated them badly, so it stirs up emotions within them. You're not a failure if someone decides they don't want to be your friend. Some people are just more compatible than others. You don't have to be liked by everyone to be a success!

For instance, Sarah was out with her friend Jenny chatting in the park when another friend of Jenny's called Alice came to join

them. Alice and Sarah had never met before but were soon getting on really well. The moment Jenny mentioned that Sarah lived in London and worked in PR, Alice's attitude towards Sarah immediately changed and she soon made her excuses and left. Sarah was left feeling confused and assumed that she'd offended Alice. She wondered what on earth she had done wrong. However, when Jenny later confronted Alice about her behaviour towards Sarah and her swift exit, she admitted that she felt insecure because Sarah was successful and glamorous, while she felt like her life, as a housewife with two kids, must have seemed incredibly mundane and dull by comparison. She was embarrassed and felt like Sarah must have been looking down on her, which, in fact, couldn't have been further from the truth. The reality was that Sarah was striving for everything that Alice had. She would have loved nothing more than to be able to meet someone and settle down herself. The reality was that Sarah was envious of Alice, yet Alice's insecurities meant she interpreted the entire situation incorrectly.

Like so many, Alice thought she had psychic ability and could perceive what Sarah thought and felt. We all do this, and 99 percent of the time this is incorrect! People not getting along often has a lot to do with miscommunication or someone stirring up other people's insecurities. So, from today, remember that if someone takes umbrage towards you, the likelihood is that it's more about *them* than it is about *you*. Don't jump to the wrong conclusion based on your initial assumptions.

We encountered a similar situation when we started appearing on TV and radio and in magazines. People we knew assumed we wouldn't want to be their friends any more because we were becoming 'celebrities'. They shied away from us without giving us a chance to show that we hadn't changed one bit and they meant as much to us as they always had. They made the decision for us that we'd changed because it stirred up negative emotions in them, whether it was jealousy, insecurity or simply feeling unsure of the relationship because of changes in our professional lives and the fact that we may leave them behind. Of course, we knew it wasn't about us as people because we were exactly the same as we'd always been.

Exercise

Write a list of all the events in your life that you consider a failure, such as a past relationship, taking too long to achieve a certain task, not passing an exam, not getting a job you'd applied for, or other similar so-called 'failures'.

Now by the side of each one write something positive that came from that experience. It could be something you learned or something you experienced or even someone new you met as a result of that experience… It may be just learning that you now know what not to do in the future, which could save you from failure again.

Affirmation

'There is always a solution to every problem. I just haven't found it yet, but I will. When I start to look I always do.'

YOUR SIXTH KEY – IT'S NEVER TOO LATE

This may sound like a crazy thing to say but it's true. Look at Colonel Sanders, who set up KFC at the age of sixty-five or Ray Kroc, who created McDonalds at the age of fifty-two.

Another example (One that is closer to home) is the story of Eva's mum. Eva is going to tell this story because it's so personal to her.

'My mum was married to my dad from the age of seventeen. As their marriage progressed, my dad would go out and socialise with his friends more and more, resulting in consuming a considerable amount of alcohol. Sadly, the alcohol would make him moody and aggressive, which my sister and I would frequently observe. They were married for almost forty years and although when he was sober he was the sweetest, kindest, funniest and gentlest man you could wish to meet, when he drank the opposite would occur and as such the consequences and ensuing arguments resulted in Mum having low self-esteem. He was opposed to mum having a career as such, and she was very dependent upon him. It appeared to me that mum

thought she was weak, worthless and couldn't live without him. When I grew up I asked her why she stayed with him and she told me she was too fearful to leave because she had no idea how she would manage on her own or financially. Furthermore, like Jekyll and Hyde, she loved the sober man, but not so when he had had a drink. However, she had never had to stand on her own two feet in any way, so she was terrified of being on her own. Like for many, the prospect of stepping out of her comfort zone was a scary prospect.

'It was hard for me to get involved because I was so close to the situation, but my mum had a few sessions with Nik and those sessions totally changed her outlook. They allowed my mum to really put her life in perspective and to begin accepting responsibility, which allowed her to take control of her life.

'Finally, she built the confidence to leave my father. Her first job was literally cleaning up in retirement homes, but she still felt incredibly proud of herself as she was making an exceptional job of surviving on her own two feet. She rented a little flat and her next major step was to start to study, and bit by bit, she built herself up.

'She was fifty-six when she left my dad. She's now seventy-two and holds a respected job, owns property, found love with a man who is younger than me and, more importantly, absolutely adores her! To me my mum is a fabulous example and inspiration. She shows more than anyone that it's never too late to change your life around. She could still be immersed in her old life, yet she has created this magical life for herself. She deserves every bit of it.'

We once treated a lady of eighty-two who suffered from emetophobia, which is the fear of vomit. At that age many people would just accept that they've suffered all their life and give up on trying to find a way to sort it out. Not this lady. She decided that enough was finally enough. We successfully treated her and she's since been away on an amazing cruise, which she had dreamed of doing all her life. At least now, no matter what her future may hold or how old she is, she can say, 'I did it.' She will have no regrets.

The point is, no one cares how old you are when you decide the moment has finally arrived to change your life. The most important thing is that you're doing it. You may do some of the things you've dreamed of most in your older years because you had fears holding you back when you were young. Once you get over those stumbling blocks – and that's all they are – you could go on to create some of your greatest memories.

Some of the world's biggest success stories didn't get to where they wanted to be until they were in their forties, fifties, sixties and so on, because they weren't ready.

We've spoken to many senior citizens, including an abundance of Nik's mum's friends, who are all eighty plus. They all agree that they have no regrets about the things they've done in their life, but they do regret the things they wanted to do but never attempted. It's vital, therefore, not to put age restrictions on yourself. Live an eventful life by creating it right now, no matter what your age.

E. L. James, who wrote *Fifty Shades of Grey*, may have wanted to write a book her entire life but lack of confidence and doubts blocked her. However, once she shifted those blocks and the time felt right, she went for it and became a multimillionaire within a couple of years at the age of forty-eight.

Just because you don't feel like you can do something *right now* doesn't mean you can never do it. Always keep in mind the old and very true saying: age ain't nothing but a number!

Exercise

You become what you think about, therefore think of yourself as a teenager! Put on some music from your youth, have a dance and allow yourself to step into your younger self to remind yourself of the energy, excitement and enthusiasm you once had.

If you've done something before, you can do it again.

Reignite the youth within yourself frequently by carrying out this exercise and listening to music from your younger years in your car, at home or on your iPod.

Affirmation

'The older I become, the more wisdom I acquire to achieve my dreams.'

YOUR SEVENTH KEY – PLAN
YOUR LIFE

I n order to change your life, you need to know what you want out of it. If you go supermarket shopping with a list, you come out with exactly what you went in there for. However, if you don't go in with a list, the chances are you'll forget the main items you went in for and will come out with a load of stuff you didn't really want.

Life is like a supermarket of choices, and there are always things there to tempt you. Essentials like potatoes, bread and eggs are purposely set far apart so you have to go down aisles laden with far more tempting goods in order to get the things you really want. Hence you come out with things you don't actually need.

Life is the same: unless you sit down and plan your life, instead of it progressing in the way that you want it to, you're going to end up laden down with things that you never really wanted, having trampled up and down the aisles of life not really getting what you dreamed of or actually deserved. And the likelihood is that on some level – no matter how deep – you already *know* what you *really* want.

If you've got a pair of blue shoes and a pair of red ones, and you ask someone which colour you should wear, you actually already know the answer yourself. You're simply asking someone else to confirm what you already know. If that person tells you to wear the blue shoes when you wanted to wear the red ones, you'll feel unhappy about it all day because you'd made the decision before you even posed the question. Therefore, you are compromising your happiness by listening to other people's opinions, despite that person not necessarily having the experience or qualifications to totally go against what you truly want. The knowledge of what you want, and what is best for you, is already inside you. Therefore, if you listen to someone else and then wear the blue shoes, the chances are you're going to feel resentful and wish you'd gone with your gut feeling at the outset.

A good example of already having the answers involves James, a workman we know. Nik tells this story.

James had been having some really bad problems with his wife. They'd been rowing a lot and he thought the relationship could be over. He talked to me about it in some detail and then said, 'What do you think?' I replied, 'Are you honestly asking me for my advice, or are you just seeking opinions? Also, who else have you asked about it?' He told me he'd asked both of his brothers and his best friend too, so I was the fourth person whose opinion he was seeking. I then asked James to tell me about the relationship status of everyone he'd asked so far. He went on to say that one of his brothers – who had never been married – had two children with two different women and was currently in an unhappy relationship with a girl who just didn't understand him; his advice to James was that his wife was not good for him and that he should leave her. His other brother – who was married and had left his wife

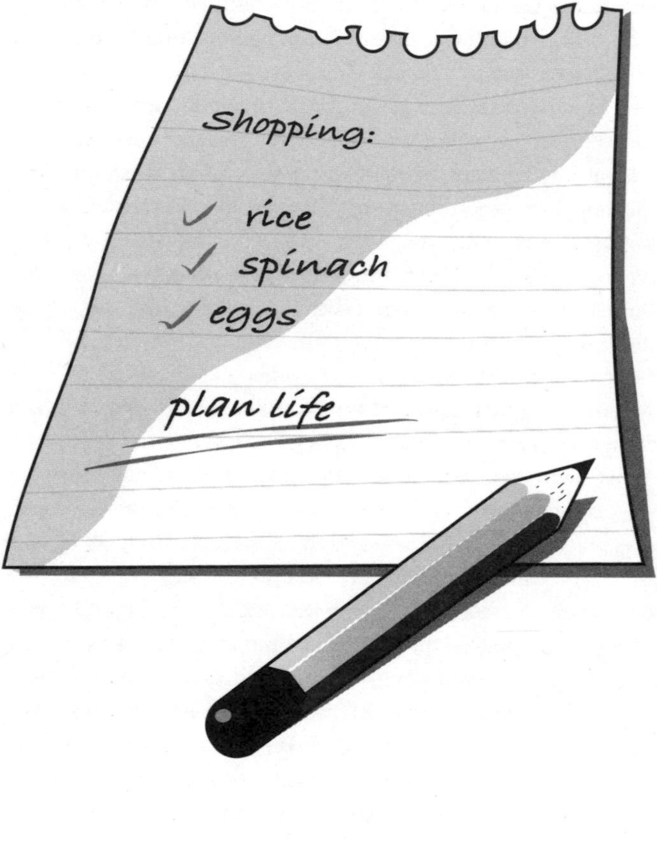
Shopping:
rice
spinach
eggs
plan life

after making a young girl pregnant – said he should go for a quiet life and just put up with it. Meanwhile, his mate – who had been with his girlfriend for a long time and was quite unhappy – said he should try and work on it, but fool around with other women to keep his options open.

I asked James to tell me about his parents' marital situation, to which he replied they had been happily married for just over fifty years. So I asked James what his parents, after all those years of marriage, had to say on the matter. He said he hadn't asked them. It was only at that moment, when I pointed out that out of all of those people he'd asked, he'd omitted to ask his parents, who were the best equipped to give him advice, that James realised where he'd been going wrong.

He had asked the advice of three people, all of whom were in bad relationships themselves. How could he possibly expect to get good advice from them, when they had all failed miserably themselves? Especially when the truth of the matter was, deep down, he already knew that he wanted to work on his relationship one last time – he just wanted someone to back him up so he felt for sure he was making the right decision.

People can ask several friends and members of their family, or even complete strangers, the same thing, but they won't be satisfied until they find someone who will back up how they already feel and give them the answer they know in their heart is the best one for them.

Most people, on an unconscious level, don't trust their own instincts even though more often than not they have the answers. They may have been taught at school or by their family how they should think, act or feel. As a result, people become indecisive because they don't trust their own judgements nearly enough.

'The clearer people are about what they want and the more focused they are on it, the more likely it is to happen. So learn to listen to yourself. No matter how much advice other people try to give you, go with your gut instinct.

We talked a bit about Arnold Schwarzenegger earlier in the book, and we're going to go into a bit more detail now because he's had such a massive impact on Nik's life.

When Nik first saw him on *The Russell Harty Show*, Arnold was promoting a film called *Pumping Iron*, but he said that from learning about the country in school his goal was always to get to America and become a movie actor. He realised to do that he had to accomplish something big to take him there. He then learned about a British bodybuilder called Reg Park, who had won Mr Universe three times and then became a star in several Hercules movies. Arnold thought he should become Mr Universe and the second Reg Park. No one else bought into his idea. In fact, his parents thought he was insane. He had pictures of Reg Park around his bed for inspiration so he could see them last thing at night and first thing in the morning, and as a result his mother called the local doctor in and had him analyse his bedroom wall as she thought there may be something terribly wrong with him. She couldn't understand why he had semi-naked men on his bedroom walls, whereas his friends all had women. Essentially, his parents couldn't comprehend how someone could be that driven to a goal they thought was unachievable. In pursuit of his goal, at the age of twenty Arnold became the youngest Mr Universe ever, beating Reg Park's record by four years. After winning it for the second time he got an invitation to go to America from Joe Weider, founder of the International Federation of Bodybuilders. Six years after he first had his dream he was in America.

He became arguably became the best bodybuilder of all time, winning Mr Olympia seven times. He's definitely the most well-known. Arnold wanted to become the highest-paid movie actor in Hollywood. In 1970 he landed his first film role and was told that no one would be able to pronounce his surname, so they stage-named him 'Arnold Strong', and just like Reg Park before him he played Hercules in a film called *Hercules in New York*. When the producers watched the initial rushes they decided that no one could possibly understand his accent, so they dubbed his voice throughout the entire film. In 1974 film director Bob Rafelson invited Arnold for an audition to read for a movie with Jeff Bridges called *Stay Hungry*, but he told Arnold he didn't want him to weigh more than 210 lb, Arnold said, 'But I have just won Mr Olympia and I am weighing 245 lb!' Bob said, 'Look, it's very simple: if you want the part, on the day we start shooting the movie I'm going to put you on the scales, and if you don't make the 210 lb you're out, because I have someone else in mind for the part.' Arnold made a decision and worked on it, visualising himself as a lean athlete in order to lose 36 lb. The day before the film was due to start shooting he was with Bob and said, 'Let's step on the scale,' and he weighed 209 lb. So it just shows that whatever you want is possible, especially if you visualise it too. Arnold went on to win a Golden Globe for his part too.

Fast-forward many years, and by the time he had completed *Terminator 3*, Arnold Schwarzenegger was the highest-paid film star in history. Did he change his name? No. Did he change his accent? No. He followed his instinct, staying true to who he was, and it was those things that got him noticed.

Arnie's other ambition had been to get into politics, and he used John F. Kennedy as a role model. Not only did he end up marrying Maria Shriver, one of Kennedy's cousins, but he also became the governor of California, the fifth-largest economy in the world. All of this happened because he planned his life.

What I really like about Arnie is how honest he is in his autobiography. Some successful people make out that their life is a magical fairy tale that happened without them having to put in any effort. They were just born brilliant! Arnie is totally honest about the fact that in following his dreams he set clear goals and nothing was left to chance. I've followed him since 1974 and I've seen how he's made life work for him, and he's nothing less than awesome.

When you come to sit down and plan your life, you can't think about 'what-ifs'. You have to really focus and believe you can achieve whatever you want to. We had our first-ever date in a huge restaurant that was in a converted historic hall. We both said how amazing it would be to live in a place like that one day. Now not only do we live in a house like that, we live in that *very* hall.

THE RETICULAR ACTIVATING SYSTEM

No matter how ridiculous something may seem, it's all within your reach once you engage something called the reticular activating system in your unconscious mind. The RAS is like a radar for all the things we want to achieve. It tells us when something is important to us and, sadly, we don't engage it enough in a positive way. Instead we tend to engage it to highlight all the stuff that is going wrong in our lives.

You'll be aware of your RAS being activated if you've ever experienced buying a new car. Think about how much time you spent on trying to find a car that's different and individual, and yet after you drive it out of the garage suddenly you start to see lots of other people driving the same car. You think, 'How did that happen? I hardly ever saw any of these cars on the road before!'

Those people haven't just bought those cars because you have, it's that your reticular activating system now sees them because they've become important to you.

A personal example of RAS that really makes me smile is when a man walked into our fitness club in 2002 looking to join. We had set up our club up five years earlier after we converted a Methodist church that had been derelict for many years. He asked how it was all going with the club, and when I replied it was going really well and each year had been better than the one before and we were now entering our fifth year, he replied, 'No you're not. That's impossible, you've only been open for about two weeks!'

We had a long conversation and he totally and utterly believed we were a brand-new club. He lived on the same road as the club and had walked past it every day going to and from work.

I asked him why he wanted to join a gym at this time, and he said that his wife had told him he was getting out of shape, so he wanted to find somewhere to exercise. It was only when he started looking around for a fitness club locally that he noticed our club, because suddenly it had become important to him. His reticular activating system had kicked in, so he picked up on it the very next time he passed by.

Some years ago we worked with a gentleman who, although he was a life coach, didn't feel entirely fulfilled by his life. We worked with him to discover things that he'd dreamed of but hadn't achieved or even considered for many years. After putting together a life plan, he went on to tell us that he was desperate to go up in a hot-air balloon. The next time we saw him, he'd done exactly that. He said to us, 'You won't believe what happened. After I saw you I went home, and when I read my local paper there was an advert for hot-air-balloon rides. How weird is that? Talk about a coincidence.'

That was no coincidence! Was that the first time that advert had been in that newspaper? No, it had probably been in there every week, but he hadn't acknowledged the article until he had engaged his reticular activating system. By telling himself that hot-air ballooning was now important to his life, his RAS picked up on the advert at that particular time simply because it was now relevant to him.

A lot of people believe in coincidences or think they're psychic because they'll think of something and then they'll see it, but it's only because your RAS is engaged and actively looking for it – like an inbuilt radar system which just needs to be switched on.

Surprisingly, most people don't even consider planning their life. They get up in the morning, they go to work, they come home and they go to bed. Then they get up and do it all again. They think having a good life relies on whether their boss decides to promote them or whether or not they get a pay rise. They're giving other people power over their lives because they're not planning them. If you want that pay rise, you need to plan it into your life and it will happen because *you* make it happen.

Most people are like leaves blowing in the wind. They might blow to a nice area and have a house and some kids, but they may blow to a slum and never meet a partner and end up miserable. People don't realise just how in charge of their lives they really are.

Similarly, when ships used to use sails to navigate, although the wind would be blowing them in so many different directions, by, firstly, having a destination and, secondly, adjusting the sails with each wind change they would always reach their destination, as opposed to going only where the wind took them. Or you could have the best cruise ship in the world, but if the captain doesn't have a clear destination, he and everyone on the ship would just end up drifting around.

We've had sessions with people and years later they've contacted us to say how well they're doing as a result of knowing what they wanted from life. One guy said his life plan was to have a Bentley. Out of the blue one day he rang us and said he wanted us to be the first people to know that that brand-new Bentley he talked about was now his and he was about to leave the showroom and drive it home. Amazing things *can* and *do* happen.

We don't believe in luck. Luck happens when preparation meets opportunity. People may say that someone who's gone on *The X Factor* and landed a record deal is lucky, but that's not down to luck. Before they even went on the show they planned to be a singer, and they may have played gigs in every small venue in the country. They also had to take action and go to *The X Factor* auditions, plan their song choices, decide what they would wear and be prepared to work incredibly hard. It's not just by chance that they've ended up there.

Other people may think they want to be a singer, but in reality they can't be bothered to get up at 5am and travel to the auditions, they don't want to spend money on a new outfit and the thought of all the work that comes with being famous feels too exhausting.

To get started, create a plan so big it even makes you feel uncomfortable, and then concentrate on one small part of it at a time. If you had to climb a mile-long staircase, the thought of getting to the top might be really exciting, and you may stay excited until you reach the bottom of the staircase. However, when you get there, the sight of it may be too overwhelming and may put you off even starting, but you don't have to climb the whole staircase straight away, all you have to do is concentrate on climbing one step. No matter how long it takes you to climb that first step, you can then focus on the next step and so on. On some level, you create everything that happens in your life. We quite simply cannot say that often enough!

Exercise

Write yourself a life plan of everything you want to achieve. You really need a very clear vision of where you want to go, and only then can you get there.

If it's meeting a perfect partner, then write down all of the attributes you want that partner to have. Be specific. It may sound cold but it's absolutely not. Imagine you're designing your perfect partner and include everything from their looks, hobbies, career to their morals and values. Writing down all these components will help you to look in the right place for your perfect partner. For example, if you're looking for someone who enjoys sport and a healthy lifestyle, then you're unlikely to find them in a nightclub.

Once you've written your list, narrow it down to a list of the top ten most important items to focus upon, then look over your list often.

To plan your life, write a list of everything you've ever wanted to do, see, be or experience. Include career, home, cars, holidays, hobbies, charities, qualifications and anything and everything you ever wished for, dreamed of, aspired to be or would regret if you never experienced or tried. Once you have an extensive list, write 1, 3, 5, 10, 15, 25 or 50 by the side of each goal, which denotes within how many years you would like to achieve that goal. You will probably find that most will be '1-year goals'.

Next just concentrate on your '1-year goals'. Take one small step on just two or three of your '1-year goals' each week. Keep a diary of what and when your next step will be. Once you've made one step, you'll notice the next step will follow naturally as it comes up in your diary. Don't overwhelm yourself. Remember, step 1 could be as simple as doing some research on the internet or making a phone call!

Affirmation

'If I don't set my own life goals, then I'll just become a part of someone else's. It's my life and I intend to live it as I see fit!'

YOUR EIGHTH KEY – YOU ARE WHAT YOU EAT

Most people have probably heard the statement 'You are what you eat.' However, very few actually hear the powerful message in those few words.

Consider that your body is a vehicle that literally drives you through life. Like a car your body needs fuel to run efficiently, it needs fuel for energy, it needs fuel to function, for your organs to work well, for your cells to regenerate, for your hair and nails to grow and, most importantly, to keep you healthy and able to fight disease.

If you add poor or polluted fuel to your vehicle, your car will run poorly, you will have a bumpy journey, parts of your car will fail or the vehicle will stop altogether. Your body is no different. The simple fact is that poor, polluted fuel or food will stop your body running efficiently. Poor food causes illness, disease, lethargy and ultimately death. Obesity, diabetes, strokes, heart disease and cancer are just a few of the diseases that have become more prevalent in today's society, and they appear to have increased at the same rate as the growth and popularity of fast-food outlets, highly processed foods, high sugar diets and dairy consumption.

Put simply, if you eat poorly, you will feel poorly, and conversely if you eat well, you will feel well. When Nik was given the prognosis of having only weeks to live, this key schema, 'You are what you eat', saved his life, and the enormity of this schema can make the difference between life and death.

Like most men, when at the young age of nineteen Nik found that he was bleeding when going to the toilet, he chose to ignore it, hoping that whatever the issue was, it would just get better. People commented that he looked very ill, gaunt and grey in colour. However, he still ignored his body trying to alert him to a serious illness. That is, until one day, when in excruciating pain, with blood pouring down his legs, he collapsed and was rushed into hospital. Having private medical insurance through work enabled Nik to seek out consultants who were considered experts in the field of gastroenterology, and he was subsequently diagnosed with chronic ulcerative colitis. In essence, Nik's colon had become so ulcerated that his colon was a mass of open ulcers and abscesses, and as a result toxins from his waste were being absorbed into his body, which would prove fatal if left untreated.

As the situation spiralled, Nik, a young man, lay in a hospital bed, being advised by a leading gastroenterologist that he had only two options: the first was to remove his bowel, which meant wearing a colostomy bag for life; the second was death. Neither option suited Nik, and he refused to accept them. With no third option, Nik sought his own.

Nik's wonderful dad had gifted him with the most incredible belief (or schema): 'There's always a way.' Believing there had to

be another option, Nik signed himself out of hospital with the determination that he would find a favourable third avenue to pursue. He left the hospital, entered the local library and, with all the energy he could muster, sat, read and educated himself on everything he could find relating to the bowel.

Following the words of Albert Einstein, who said that simplicity is genius, Nik looked for a simple solution. In the first instance, knowing that the colon is a passage for waste, Nik stopped eating. He figured that to allow the sores to heal, he should stop waste passing through, which he felt would aggravate the ulcers. Within a week he noted an improvement and continued with a clear-liquid diet. Over the following weeks, as Nik's health improved and the bleeding subsided, he slowly started to introduce one food at a time, and noted how good foods such as brown rice and vegetables caused no reaction, yet fibrous foods and wheat products would cause irritation.

However, the biggest realisation for Nik, one that literally made him well, came when he acknowledged the biggest catalysts aggravating his condition were dairy products. Being an avid weight trainer over the two years before his illness, Nik had increased his dairy consumption significantly. He was mixing protein powder with a glass of milk three times a day.

When we met, Eva was a considerable dairy fan, and as a vegetarian her diet consisted of a significant quantity of cheese, yoghurt and milky drinks. Eva had suffered from IBS as a teenager, with a combination of symptoms from bloating and urgency to use the toilet to constipation or diarrhoea. IBS-type symptoms can be created by the production of adrenalin too, and having a home life with a significant level of anxiety also contributed to her IBS. However, after Nik shared his negative experience with dairy products, she too stopped consuming them and was shocked at how quickly the IBS symptoms and bloating passed.

Without wanting to make this chapter about dairy, suffice to say we are a non-dairy yet very healthy household, consuming only almond or coconut milk. Together we have studied the effects of cows' milk, which is obviously specifically produced for a baby cow, to take it from a small calf of approximately 63 lb at birth to a full-grown cow of 1,500 lb over a period of only two years. Coupled with the hormones, antibiotics and growth hormones that dairy cows are given, this is not a great combination for a human, who takes up to twenty years to grow to their full size.

Interestingly, we are the only animal, that drinks another animal's breast milk. Many people feel repulsed at the thought of drinking a cup of tea made with human breast milk, yet we don't hesitate to ingest liquid excreted from a cows' udders. Many of these cows suffer from mastitis and crusty infected nipples from the harsh suckers that extract their milk. This leads to cows being pumped with antibiotics and hormones, which then transfer to the milk that humans drink.

At the time of writing, the country with the second-largest dairy product consumption in the world is France, and France happens to have the highest rate of cancer also. Interestingly, China does not appear among the fifty countries with the highest levels of cancer. Although these findings may appear somewhat controversial, the Western world has slowly started to realise the negative effects of dairy, and as such a whole host of alternatives have sprung up in supermarkets such, as soya milk, rice milk, coconut milk, almond milk, cashew milk and hazelnut milk.

We have researched and come across many examples of people whose health has improved as a result of cutting dairy out of their diet, but we have also come across a staggering number of cases of people being told they were terminally ill, only to regain full health as a result of removing dairy from their diet immediately. One such case that stood out for us was that of Professor Jane Anne Plant CBE.

Jane was a leading geochemist, scientist and author and Professor of Geochemistry at Imperial College London. In 1993, she was told she only had months to live after her breast cancer returned for a fifth time. As a married mum of young children who had just gone through several surgeries, thirty-five radiotherapy treatments, irradiation to induce the menopause and chemother-apy treatments, she was devastated. Jane had a lump the size of half a boiled egg sticking out of her neck. She was thin, pale and looked and felt awful. However, her scientific knowledge and experience thankfully saved her life.

In the past, Jane and her husband Peter had both worked in China, and Jane recalled being shown an epidemiological atlas. This showed an incredibly low breast cancer rate of one in every 100,000 women in China, whereas in the Western world at the time the rate was a staggering one in ten. Jane confirmed these statistics with senior academics she knew well in China and also Chinese doctor colleagues, who confirmed that they had hardly ever seen a case of breast cancer in their career.

Understandably, this ignited an interest. Jane knew of Chinese women living on Western diets in Britain who did have breast cancer, yet in China there was a negligible number. As a consequence she asked her husband the question that literally saved her life: 'Why don't Chinese women in China get breast cancer?' Together they considered every eventuality, and then Jane's husband remembered that when working in China, his Chinese colleagues had given him some powdered cow's milk on a field expedition as they did not drink it themselves. It was the early 1980s and China did not even have a dairy industry.

Jane decided she had nothing to lose so she would stop eating dairy immediately, and instantly cut out the low fat organic yoghurts she had eaten daily for some time. Miraculously, within only six weeks the cancer disappeared, and she then adopted a non-dairy, vegan diet and remained free of cancer for nineteen years.

Almost twenty years later, Jane started to write an academic book, and this proved demanding. She found she was being less careful with her diet, having the occasional sandwich from the college canteen, which invariably contained butter or spread, and she stopped checking herself for any lumps or anomalies. Her husband then noticed a lump under her collarbone. It was cancer and had spread to the lining of her right lung. Jane realised she had been less careful with her diet, and checked with the college canteen what she had been eating. She was shocked to learn that even the falafel from the canteen contained milk powder. She had also been eating calves' liver cooked in butter about three times a month at a local restaurant.

Jane went back to her non-dairy and vegan diet, adding meditation and complementary therapies to help her relax. In less than six months, Jane was once more cancer-free and thankfully in remission. Jane remained free from cancer from thereon in, passing away in her seventies from an aneurysm.

Jane is just one of many people who changed their lives by changing their diet, just like Nik.

Exercise

Have two weeks avoiding ALL dairy and note how you feel. You can then add simple sugars to your 'avoid' list for a further two weeks, and then add gluten for two more weeks after that.

Take some 'before' and 'after' photos and measurements of your stomach and waist, and a side-on photo of your tummy so you can observe any reduction in bloating. Also take photos of your hair and skin and note the difference after six weeks free from dairy, sugar and gluten. Be sure to speak with your GP if you have any health conditions that may be affected by removing gluten from your diet.

Affirmation

'I really am what I eat. Therefore I will eat healthily and I will become healthy.'

YOUR NINTH KEY – SAVE YOURSELF BEFORE YOU SAVE THE WORLD

To a certain extent we are all people-pleasers, so we like to do stuff for other people before we look after ourselves. However, you simply have to put yourself first. If you spend your life looking after your husband or wife and children but you don't look after yourself, you could end up getting ill, and then not being able to look after anyone. However, if you put aside time for yourself to go to the gym or get a massage or whatever makes you feel good, you'll be in a much better place to take care of your loved ones because you'll be fit and healthy both mentally and physically.

We've seen so many people in our therapy sessions who have given so much they've got nothing left to give.

A good analogy to remind you of the importance of putting yourself first is thinking about the procedure when you take a flight on a plane. The flight attendants always tell you that if the air pressure drops, you must put your own mask on before you help anyone else. So many people fall by the wayside because they're trying so hard to put masks on everyone else that they run out of air themselves. You have to administer oxygen to yourself before you can help and support anyone else.

Think of how many mothers run themselves into the ground looking after their family. But if they die early from illness as a result, thereby leaving their children without a mother, their children will suffer ten times more.

Society tells us that putting ourselves first sometimes is selfish, but the reality is that it's the complete opposite. You can't look after other people unless you can look after yourself.

Personally, we very rarely have to take time off work, or let people down due to illness, because we look after ourselves well and if we weren't in peak health we wouldn't be able to look after our patients and children anywhere near as well as we need to. Therefore, our diary, appointments, social life and business trips are organised around keeping fit and eating healthily, with a 'cheat' or 'dirty' day built in once in every week.

Why should you compromise what you want for the sake of others? It doesn't make you a bad person if you make yourself happy.

If you keep putting everyone before yourself, you'll end up feeling frustrated, angry and resentful, and you can't be a great friend or parent if you're feeling that way. A great example of this is a friend of ours called Emma. She always used to put everyone else's thoughts and feelings before her own, to the point where she didn't even stop and question what she was about to agree to. She would just say 'yes' to something because it was her default setting. She thought that in order to be liked she had to keep everyone else happy all of the time, even though it meant making herself unhappy.

Not too long ago, Emma's friend Ailsa asked if she could come

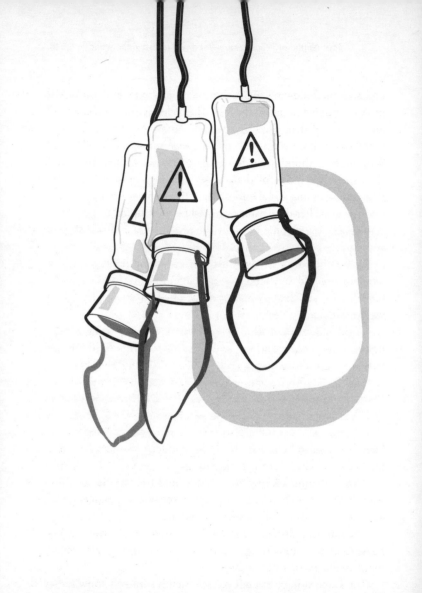

and stay the following night. Emma's spare room was filled with junk she needed to put in the loft. The bed sheets needed changing, and on top of that, she had a friend coming for dinner the same night with whom she was keen to spend some one-on-one time. Without even thinking she told Ailsa it was fine for her to stay and then spent the whole of that evening feeling angry about all the effort it was going to take to prepare the room for her guest. She was also cross her dinner plans would be interrupted.

After giving it some thought she texted Ailsa and said she was very sorry, but it wasn't convenient for her to stay after all, and she explained the reasons. Ailsa texted back saying it wasn't a problem as she could stay somewhere else and she wasn't in the least bit offended and understood it was a bit of a pain in view of the circumstances.

Emma had wasted all of that time and energy getting worked up, upset and stressed when all she had to do was stop, think, put herself first and say 'no', which was perfectly understandable in view of the circumstances.

We tend to build things up so much and often think for other people. Emma had convinced herself that Ailsa would be cross if she said she couldn't stay. Her head was swimming with thoughts like: 'She'll be so offended. She'll think I don't like her. She won't like me as much. I'll really let her down.'

How did Emma know how Ailsa would feel? Could she mind-read? Even if Ailsa had been a bit upset, she would soon get over it and, as it turned out, she didn't mind one bit.

The amazing thing is that once you start to put yourself first regularly, you'll find it easier and easier. The saying 'yes' default mode is a habit that can be broken.

Think about it, you've got certain friends who you know if they say 'no' to a party invitation, then they mean '*no*'. However, you have other friends who although they may initially say 'no', you know they will cave in if you apply a little pressure. It's the ones who say 'no' and mean it that we have the most respect for, and therefore we don't push our luck with them. Wouldn't you rather be the person people respect as opposed to being the pushover?

Once Emma started being more honest with herself and said 'no' to things more often, she became a lot happier and more relaxed. If someone was offended because she didn't fall into line with everything they expected from her, that was their issue. You can't keep everyone happy all of the time. Certainly not without making yourself unhappy.

Emma also came to the realisation that a big part of the reason she was single was because she was so busy looking after everyone else. There was no room for a man in her life.

It suddenly struck her that on a deeper level she was worried what her friends would think if she weren't available 24/7 like she had been. Surely she would upset her friends and potentially lose them at the cost of her happiness? Ironically, all the friends were in relationships, but would call on Emma if their partners were out for the night. If she had a boyfriend, she would have no choice but to turn down invitations because she wouldn't have the time to fit everything in, and then what would happen to those friendships? Simple. The people who mattered would stick around, and those who only really liked Emma because everything was on their terms would fall by the wayside – proving that they were very unhealthy, very one-sided friendships to start with.

J. K. Rowling is someone who took a long time to put herself first, but once she did, it paid off for her and her family in a huge way. She was a single mother and probably used to doing everything for other people and not giving herself much time and care. When she came to write *Harry Potter*, she used to sit in a café pushing her pram with her foot to keep her baby soothed.

Some people may have looked at her and thought she was really selfish for having a baby lying next to her for hours on end while she wrote, but the reality was that she was saving herself and creating a future for her family.

If she had never allowed herself the space to start writing *Harry Potter*, her life, and that of her children, would have been very different. In fact, she may have ended up unhappy and resentful towards the children because she wasn't fulfilling her ambitions. By putting herself first for that short period of time, she not only helped herself and her family, she also helped an incredible amount of other people through her charity work, while making millions of others incredibly happy through her fantastic storytelling.

We had a patient called Ruth who had terrible depression the first time we met her. She had two daughters who were also miserable because she was always so unhappy at home. She'd been to her doctor to get medication and had been thinking about getting therapy for some time, but she kept thinking about how the money could go towards a new coat or school shoes for one of her daughters.

One day, her husband told her she had to do something about her moods because their marriage was in danger of breaking down. She started to see that she would lose everything if she didn't invest in herself.

We helped her break through the negative pattern of depression she had fallen into and learn to look after herself. Ruth now has a really good career that involves her going into offices to coach people. As a result her marriage has improved dramatically, she and her husband have been able to move house, they've got nicer cars, they go on holiday and the whole family are much happier. She even sent us an email from Australia saying that she was finally experiencing the world. That's all as a consequence of making a decision, taking action and then putting herself first.

Exercise
Close your eyes. See an image of yourself in front of you in your mind's eye. Make the image of yourself happy, confident, strong and healthy. Make that image big, bright, clear and colourful. Grab that image as if giving it a hug. Hold yourself close, and notice how great that feels. Hold it for a few seconds, keeping that feeling growing, then open your eyes. Do this exercise at least twice each week and notice your inner power grow. Write a reminder for yourself in your diary, so you don't overlook yourself amid the hustle and bustle of daily life.

Affirmation
'The only person who will be with me twenty-four hours a day, seven days a week for the rest of my life is ME. I owe it to myself and for the benefit of those around me to put myself FIRST.'

YOUR TENTH KEY – THERE ARE NO BAD PEOPLE IN THE WORLD

For obvious reasons this statement creates a lot of debate. However, please consider this: while there are no bad people in the world, sometimes people (often good people), because of circumstances, can do bad things.

We like to use the film *Trading Places* as an example of what we mean, as this film highlights a well-known debate known as 'nature versus nurture'. From a psychological point of view the film proves that there are no bad people. Only bad circumstances make people bad.

The movie shows that you can put the most upstanding person, like the character Winthorpe in the film, a successful and wealthy commodities broker, into a terrible situation and he'll become what's perceived to be a bad person, in Winthorpe's case having to steal to survive. Meanwhile, Valentine, a homeless beggar, also has his life turned around, becoming a better person as a result of being put into more plush surroundings, given responsibility and

respect and, therefore, increased self-esteem.

If a person ended up on the streets – no matter how good they were to start with – and the only way they could survive was by stealing food, they would steal food. If you're in a life or death situation and you're being attacked, you will attack back and potentially become a murderer, but you are not a murderer, and in view of the mitigating circumstances you are not a bad person either. It's human nature.

It works the other way as well. Someone can grow up in a terrible environment, but it just takes one person to invest in them and show them that trust exists and they can turn their lives around.

Consider this: a young black American woman born into poverty in rural Mississippi to a teenage mother, who left her for her first six years of life. She was so poor she wore dresses made from potato sacks.

She was raped from the age of nine by numerous family members and then ran away from home aged thirteen, becoming pregnant at the age of fourteen. Her son died in infancy.

She then went to live with the man she believed to be her father, who was strict but ensured she had a high standard of education.

She has two half-sisters: one was adopted, the other died of a cocaine overdose. And she has a half-brother who has AIDS.

Anyone looking at that situation would expect this woman to have a bleak future ahead, but this is the story of Oprah Winfrey. It's amazing testimony to the worst possible circumstances any individual could face being totally turned around.

Of course, there are exceptions to every rule, and when we've talked about there being no bad people in the world at our seminars people in the audience have opposed our belief and asked, for example, how can we say that suicide bombers aren't bad people?

Those people weren't *born* bad, they grew up in an environment where they were brought up to believe that Westerners are the enemy. They think the way to honour their family is to protect them by killing as many Westerners (or 'infidels') as possible.

If you're brought up with that belief and it's all you know, you don't question it. Quite simply, you don't know any better. They're not bad people and they were not born with the intention of killing others; they have bad beliefs and an incredible amount of fear taught to them. It's a simple formula. We are all a product of our environment and we simply copy behaviour.

If someone were to adopt a child who was born into the Taliban and that child was brought up with our beliefs and values, they would be very different. Not only would they have different beliefs, but they would also speak a different language and have an entirely different palate. We're all a product of our environment and there is always a positive intent in everything we do. If we believe that family honour and saving 'our' people is a positive thing, we'll do whatever we can to uphold that.

It's all about learned behaviour, and sadly people can grow up with good and bad examples to varying degrees. Obviously, not all learned behaviour leads to something as extreme as someone becoming a terrorist, but what we learn has an impact on us forever, unless we challenge and then begin to change those behaviours, by conditioning them with new evidence and thoughts.

Sure, there is a small percentage of people who don't want to change and who like behaving badly, as there are exceptions to every rule. However, there are far less of them than you think. If you took a bad person and put them in good circumstances, the chances are you would see a change just like in the film *Trading Places*. Likewise, if you put a good person in bad circumstances, the chances are they would change for the worse because they would have to fight to survive.

If, however, you believe that there are loads of bad people in the world who make it a horrible place, it's not them who are suffering, it's you. The moment Eva forgave the person who had bullied her, and understood that she tried to belittle her due to her own insecurities and low self-esteem, she was able to let go of the notion that the bully was pure evil or bad in some way, and that the bullying was personal. The fact is, the bully would always find someone to bully, and it just happened to be Eva. Just by doing that Eva felt better about herself because she knew she had never done anything to purposely hurt or antagonise the bully. By empathising with her bully, she empathised with herself, and only then did the bullying and its effects end.

If you believe people are bad, it's like mixing up a poison for someone else and drinking it yourself because you're the one who's going to feel sick and angry. Those negative feelings won't affect them, but they will make you unhappy and bitter.

If you do perceive someone to have a negative effect on you through their actions, you have a choice whether or not you want to see that person.

You need to take a step back and consider how other people can affect the way you feel, especially if you are trying to change things to get a more positive outcome in the long term.

Two of our cats, Arnie and Banks, get fleas and ticks, so we give them a treatment and within forty-eight hours they are tick- and flea-free. While the treatment lasts two months, if they kept away from fleas and ticks they would never need another application. However, as they like going over to the farm near our house and playing with the farm cats, all of which have fleas, guess what? Yes, as soon as the treatment wears off in two months they get fleas and ticks again, and subsequently need treating again too.

Cats are no different to people. You can work on yourself time and time again and take massive steps forward, but if you still surround yourself with negative people who are determined to pull you back, it's equivalent to playing with a cat with fleas. Make no mistake, negative people will contaminate you and your world, therefore it's vital you consider your social circles. If you keep going back to the same circles hoping for a different outcome, the likelihood is that unless *they've* changed (never mind you), you'll be flea-ridden again before you know it.

It's important to also be aware that not everyone may love the positive, happy new you. Often people don't like to see their friends or family changing because they're comfortable with who they perceive them to be, especially if the changes affect them in ways they're not happy with.

If a brother is used to being able to push his sister around and manipulate her into doing what he wants, then all of a sudden that sister is standing up for herself, the brother won't like it one little bit. Why should he have to go and visit their sick grandma when she can do it? Why should he have to buy a birthday present for their dad when she can get it while she's buying hers? The brother's schema may be that the sister will always do what he wants, so he is less than happy when that's challenged.

On top of that, the people around you may even feel jealous of you because they don't feel like they're moving on with their lives or making positive changes in the same way.

It may be that you have to take a very long look at the people you surround yourself with, and you can no longer be around those who don't have your best interests at heart. At least until they've accepted that the new you isn't going to magically morph back into the passive person you were before.

The happier and more positive you feel, the more you'll notice who is good for you and who isn't. Part of saving yourself is moving away from people who contaminate you, in whatever negative form that takes. Just consider, if you have five friends who smoke, then you are likely to smoke too, just as if you have five friends who are broke or unhappy, then you will be the sixth. When you consider this you realise how important it is to surround yourself with people not like who you are, but like who you want to be.

We put people into three categories – supporters, igniters and draggers. Supporters are friends and family who do exactly that, support you no matter what. Whatever you do, right or wrong, they are always there for you and are not judgemental.

Igniters are rare and often hard to find, but when you find one they are wonderful. They're the people who make you feel like you are amazing and can do anything, and they encourage you, push you forward and always want the best for you.

Lastly, there are the draggers, who are the people who bring you down. A great test to ascertain who the draggers in your life are is when your mobile phone rings: you go to pick it up, see the name of the caller on your phone, and you slump and get that *'oh no'* feeling. In fact, not only do you often not take the call, but you have to build up energy to find the right time to call them back. This instantly tells you that that person isn't good for you. They zap positive energy and self-belief out of you.

No matter how many times we tell you all of the simple but amazing ways you can make your life better, if you still hang around with people who breed negativity, they will keep pulling you back.

To conclude, this schema, which generally proves the most difficult to accept for many people, is not about the bad people in the world or their actions. In fact, it's not about them at all. It's about you! This schema is all about allowing you to let go of the anger or resentment you may have towards those who have wronged you, and encouraging you to consider the actions of others more before passing judgement on them, which in turn will make your world a less constricted and brighter place.

Exercise

Take the mobile phone test.

Look through your list of contacts and imagine how you would feel if a certain person were to call you? If you have any shred of reluctance, dread or negativity, then you can safely define that person as a dragger and you need to make a decision to distance yourself from them.

Conversely, look at the ones who you would always be happy to speak to, those who on just hearing their voice make you feel immediately better, and make a point of speaking to them more often. They are supporters or igniters, and they are positive, not negative, influences on your life.

Affirmation

'Bad people aren't born, they're merely victims themselves, created by bad circumstances and beliefs. I will actively seek out igniters while avoiding draggers.'

YOUR ELEVENTH KEY – YOU'VE GOT TO GIVE TO RECEIVE

We were very confused when we first heard about the concept of giving to receive. We couldn't understand how giving your money away could generate more. We thought of it in terms of material possessions. Then one day the reality of this statement hit Nik, and he's going to tell this story.

I would often hear our son Hunter tell Eva that he loved her, but he never told me. Every night when Hunter went to bed Eva would tell him she loved him, and he would say the same back. As Hunter never told me, one day I said to him, 'Do you love your dad?' He replied, 'Of course I do.'

I came from a family where my dad never told me he loved me, but he did absolutely everything for me so it went without saying. I just *knew*. I copied that behaviour and was doing the same with Hunter and therefore got the same result. You see, my dad never told me he loved me, nor I him, but of course we both did.

I decided to change my behaviour, and I started to tell Hunter

every night that I loved him. After two weeks, very randomly as we were walking along he took my hand and said, 'I love you, Dad.'

That would never have happened if I hadn't changed the way I had been, and it's amazing how quickly things can turn around. Every day since we tell each other.

It's incredible how giving to charity or doing kind things for people comes back to you. Even just giving someone a smile in the street can make a massive difference. Think how good you feel when someone smiles or says hello to you for no reason. You can be walking down a busy street and feeling grumpy about the fact there are so many people around. Then, if you bump into someone and they smile or make a light-hearted comment about how crowded it is or give you a simple compliment like, 'I love your coat,' it can put a little spring in your step. You definitely get back what you put out. You can very easily change someone's day with just a kind word.

It works the same way with compliments. If you have the mind-set that whenever you see someone you're going to find something positive about them and then give them a compliment, it can stay with them for days. Furthermore, you will feel great for making someone happy, and that feeling is priceless. You'll also find that they may even compliment you back too, so it's a huge win–win situation! Let's face it, who doesn't love that?

The same thing happens when naughty children get told they'll never amount to anything by intolerant, fed-up teachers. Although it's a throwaway comment, that child soaks up those harsh words and may grow up thinking they're always going to be a failure. That ill-thought-out remark can sink into the unconscious and create a schema that could negatively impact that child's life forevermore.

This is where we go back to the third schema of accepting responsibility – only you can challenge and change those thoughts and realise that they are wrong.

The thing to remember is that the world is like a mirror, so everything you put out will come back to you eventually.

Whatever people think about Simon Cowell, he gives and receives like a pro. Some people think he's a money-making machine or they're jealous of his success, but he's given a lot of people a lot of opportunities. Some of the people who have appeared on his shows would never have got the chance to leap into the limelight or get a record deal otherwise. Whether you agree with the way he works or not, it's hard not to feel inspired by him on some level. If there's one man who believes in himself and knows that he'll have an even more successful future, it's Simon Cowell.

If we're looking at the schema of giving to receive from a material or monetary point of view, the example we like to give relates to when we first set up our business. We knew we wanted to help people and, at first, we saw a lot of clients for free. As a result, they recommended us to people, who then came along and paid us for therapy.

We still treat some people for free to this day, and if we see someone in the street who is suffering, we will always offer to help if we have the time to stop. The big payback from that is we get an absolutely amazing feeling. We love seeing people happy, so we will always do what we can to make that happen.

Exercise

Smile, give compliments, make an effort to speak to people at work you'd normally ignore and compliment them on their contribution. Unexpectedly tell your partner, children, family and friends you love them, call an old aunt to see how she is, buy or donate something to the local charity shop. Do as many things as you can to make your world a nicer place and then reap the emotional rewards.

Affirmation

'My world is a mirror. What I put out will reflect back at me. I put out love, kindness, gratitude and success.'

YOUR TWELFTH KEY – YOU BECOME WHAT YOU THINK ABOUT

Albert Einstein said, 'Imagination is more important than knowledge. For knowledge is limited to all we now know and understand, while imagination embraces the entire world.'

Schema number twelve basically sums up all of the others. It also leads on from number eleven very neatly, only in this chapter we're talking about the negative messages that we give ourselves on a daily basis.

If you believe that you'll never amount to anything, the chances are you won't. If you think you're the ugly one, you will be. Harsh, but true.

At the other end of the scale, there are some people who may not be that talented or good-looking but they think they're better than everyone else, hence developing a superiority complex. Given a choice between the two, the superiority complex will win out every time for us. Although it's taking things to the extreme and we certainly don't advocate it, at least if you think you're incredible you won't care what other people say about you anyway, thus providing a cast-iron emotional shield. Whereas those people who feel inferior will be so fragile they'll get hurt and walked over time and time again.

The real trick is to find the middle ground, to be happy with yourself, without being arrogant. There is definitely a very fine line between self-belief and arrogance!

Lucy is thirty-seven, pretty and a statuesque size sixteen. She knows she's not perfect and she's never going to be a size eight, but she wakes up every day happy – because she is happy with herself.

As she said to us: 'People may not walk into a room and think I'm the thinnest or the prettiest girl in there. They may not turn their heads and gasp when I walk past, but as soon as I start a conversation with someone I win them over because I'm fun to be around. I don't carry around a "Poor me, I'm not skinny" attitude, I embrace what I've got, and as a result I'm great company. I've never found it difficult to attract men and have often found myself laughing the night away with the most attractive man at a party, while a model-esque girl stands in the corner on her own pouting miserably. Friends who I deem to be beautiful ask *me* for lessons in pulling. It's hilarious.

'I don't hanker to be anything other than what I am. I learned a long time ago not to try and be the impossible. I just want to be the best me I can be, and that means embracing my flaws as well as my attributes and my dark side as well as my light.'

Lucy is a perfect example. Your thoughts create your world, so if you change your thoughts and actions, you can totally change your life. The process of using these twelve key schemas is all about changing your thought patterns. If you say you won't ever trust

anyone again, you won't let anyone into your world. But if you tell yourself you *do* trust people, you'll be letting in the good ones. Yes, there may well be a dodgy few here and there. Part of The Key, as we've mentioned earlier in the book, is you have a *choice* as to who you have in your life.

There's a proverb that says, 'Prepare for the worst but hope for the best.' That's not telling you to be negative, it's just saying that some bad things may happen, but always expect the best anyway.

Really think about the way you say things and notice the effect certain words have on you. If you are slightly annoyed about something, but tell your friend that you're 'absolutely furious', you will end up feeling that level of anger. Think about what happens when someone tells you that you look tired. You immediately feel tired, don't you? If you're bunking off work when you're actually totally fine, you often end up feeling ill because on an unconscious level you're telling yourself you are.

Thoughts and emotions create physical symptoms in the same way they create our future, which is why it's so important to be aware of how you're feeling when you say things. You can totally change a situation by changing your emotional reaction to it. For instance, if someone purposely steals the last car parking space right from under your nose, you can either get so cross you feel your heart pounding and the beginnings of a headache, or you can take a deep breath and think how awful it must be to be the kind of person who would do something so mean. Who's the winner then?

It's much the same with worry. Worry is nothing more than a down payment on a loan that very rarely will you ever take out.

Our friend Simon lives in a flat in London. He's been there for five years and the flat below him has been empty the entire time. He's asked the owner to do something about it but he keeps putting him off, so he's decided not to worry about it for now. He's discovered that actually it's quite nice that he can make noise and no one complains.

However, his mum is constantly worrying that squatters are going to move in, and every time she speaks to Simon she reminds him that it will be harder for him to sell the flat if the downstairs one is an empty mess. Simon's reply is, 'I'm not planning on moving for a while, Mum, so why worry about something which I don't need to be concerned with? The owner could choose to do it up tomorrow and everything will be fine. If he doesn't, I'll cross that bridge when I come to it, otherwise it's wasted energy.'

There is no point in Simon spending the next few years getting worked up and stressed about something that he can't do anything about and isn't affecting his life in a negative way right now. In fact, the constant nagging from his mum was more stressful than the problem itself, before he politely asked her to stop asking him about it!

The best example we can possibly give of thoughts creating things is the story of Nik's close friend.

She has always been a really outgoing woman with wild red hair, a full face of make-up and a great sense of humour. She always looked after herself well and was the life and soul of every party.

One day she got a cough that wouldn't go away, and following some tests she was diagnosed with lung cancer. Doctors told her that, coupled with her advancing age, it was too aggressive for them to do anything about, so they told her to go off and enjoy the rest of her life.

Overnight she became what she thought she was – a woman who was dying of cancer. She stopped going out and putting on make-up, and she lost her appetite, and therefore lost a lot of weight. She had no energy and her family felt like they were watching her die right in front of their eyes.

Two months later, she got a phone call asking her to go to the hospital urgently. When she saw the doctor he turned to her and said, 'I'm so, so sorry. We mixed up your X-rays with someone else's and you actually had pleurisy, and you don't have cancer.'

Within days she transformed from a frail, dying, weak cancer victim and was back to her old fun-loving, flamboyant self with her make-up back on, chatting and laughing with friends and loving life. Had she not been told that she didn't have cancer, who's to say she wouldn't have died anyway, because she had effectively given up on life? The minute she knew she wasn't dying, she started living again. The change in her was nothing short of incredible.

One of our friends, Alan, was telling us about his grandmother, who always looked amazing for her age. However, the minute she turned sixty, she literally aged overnight.

To her that was 'old age', and she was constantly churning out the mantra, 'Well of course I can't do that, I'm sixty now, you know.'

Alan said that not only did he see an emotional change in his gran in the years that followed that milestone birthday, but physically she went from looking incredible and youthful to turning into a little old lady. It was as if turning sixty had given her the excuse she wanted to give up on life and have everyone running around after her feeling sorry for her. What a waste of a life!

The bottom line is, we believe what we're told. If you look at everything from voodoo to witchcraft, even though there is no scientific proof whatsoever, many, many people are convinced that these mystical practices work. As a result of these misguided beliefs, if you went up to someone who believes in voodoo and told them you'd put a spell on them and they're going to get very ill as a result, the likelihood is that they will. This would not be as a result of any imaginary spell, but because of the suggestion, the fear and the fact that their belief is so strong.

Look at how many people are convinced that Tarot readers can predict the future. Firstly, we are all the masters of our own destiny and we can make decisions and take action to entirely alter our current path in life. Secondly, if someone we have total faith in tells us something we want to believe in, we will go out of our way to make it happen, whether it's consciously or unconsciously. That's just another form of planning your life. If you believe without question that what someone is telling you is true, you're focusing all of your energies on that. As we know, that's incredibly powerful because it activates the brain's reticular activating system, which, as we discussed earlier, works just like radar or putting a destination into your satellite navigation system in your car. We have already said every acorn has an oak tree within it. Just like the oak tree, if you want to grow to your full potential, you have to start thinking like an oak and not an acorn, you have to start thinking like the person you want to become, not the person you currently are.

Let's look at what kinds of 'I am' statements come out of your mouth, as these can totally affect your life and how you behave. So what do you say? I am a failure, I am never any good, I am useless, I am difficult, I am undisciplined, I am unattractive, I am always making mistakes, I am depressed?

You should never say negative things about yourself. No one would approach someone and say those things to their face, and yet, remarkably, we often have no problem saying those things to ourselves. Negative thoughts actually curse your future. Let's be honest here, you may have enough in life against you already, without being against yourself too. So if you change your 'I am' statements you can take your life to a whole new level. Consider using, I am grateful, I am talented, I am victorious, I am blessed, I am strong, I am amazing, I am attractive, I am successful, I am free, I am kind, I am confident. Always make sure that you have the right 'I am's coming out of your mouth. The new 'I am's may not feel true for you right now, but you have to read them and say them out loud as if they already were. Keep doing this and one day you will suddenly wake up and feel amazing and realise exactly just how amazing you are.

Our final incredible example of becoming what you think about is a story of a young boy who walked up to McLaren Formula One team boss Ron Dennis, asked him for his autograph and said, 'Hi, I'm Lewis Hamilton. I won the British Championship [karting cadet class] and one day I want to be racing your cars.' Ron signed Lewis's autograph book, telling him to call him in nine years' time and they'd sort something out. In reality, just a few years later, he was officially signed to the McLaren Driver Development Support Programme, becoming the youngest driver ever to have been contracted by an F1 team.

This boy's dream started after receiving a radio-controlled car from his dad when he was six years of age and becoming obsessed with racing. As a result, his father bought him his first go-kart as a Christmas present and told him that he would support his racing career as long as he worked hard at school. It didn't take Lewis long to start winning, and he won his first British go-karting championship at the age of eight. Aged twenty-two, Lewis started driving F1 for McLaren in 2007. In his debut race in Australia he finished third, becoming the thirteenth driver to finish on the podium in his first F1 race. Later in the season Lewis had both his first pole position and first victory of his F1 career at the Canadian Grand

Prix in Montreal. A week later he won the United States Grand Prix, becoming the first Briton since John Watson in 1983 to win an F1 race in the US, and only the second person, after Jacques Villeneuve, to win more than one race in his rookie F1 season. Remarkably, at the end of his debut season Lewis ended up only one point behind that year's champion, the seasoned professional Kimi Räikkönen. In addition to placing second in his debut season Lewis also recorded nine consecutive podium finishes, more than any other rookie in F1 history.

The following season Lewis clinched the F1 World Championship, becoming the youngest driver to win the title. He was also the first British driver to win the World Championship since Damon Hill, who triumphed in 1996.

Lewis went on to win two more F1 world titles in 2014 and 2015, and then in 2017 he broke another record at the Italian Grand Prix when he secured his 69th pole position, surpassing the great Michael Schumacher for most pole positions. During qualifying for the United States Grand Prix, Lewis won his 72nd pole position and his 117th front row start, setting a new record for front row starts, surpassing Schumacher's previous record.

Lewis went on to win the 2017 F1 World Championship, racking up his fourth title win and becoming the best British F1 driver in history, joining Sebastian Vettel and Alain Prost as a four-time World Championship winner, leaving only two drivers in the world with more titles: Juan Manuel Fangio, with five, and the great Michael Schumacher, with an almighty seven. With Lewis continuing to race, however, who knows what may happen, and how exciting that he could end up being the best F1 driver in history. Thankfully, Lewis's dad believed and supported the dreams of that six-year-old boy who became exactly what he thought about.

You don't need to go to a Tarot reader to predict your future – you can predict it by choosing it and creating it yourself.

Exercise

Imagine you are writing a movie script and creating the perfect character that you want and need to be to fulfil your dreams.

Write a list of your perfect character's mannerisms and attitudes and, just like a movie role, rehearse and then perform them, first in your mind, then alone to a mirror and then in real-life situations.

Practice makes perfect and you will be able to adopt these new, far more empowering behaviours in everyday life. At first this will be conscious and require effort; however, with practice, this will become habitual and effortless. Make a list of at least ten 'I am's and read them often throughout the day, saying them out loud and meditating on them.

Affirmation

'Anything is possible and I can be whatever I choose to be, as I am and will always be invincible.'

IT'S TIME TO TAKE ACTION

Okay, so we have shared with you how we managed to totally transform our lives, and we have also shared the twelve key schemas that allowed us to, and that will also allow YOU to do the same.

You now have the tools and also some amazing examples of how some people, perhaps just like you, have totally turned their lives around.

Now it's your turn.

We've never tried to impress anyone with what we have personally achieved, but we do try and impress *upon* people that just like us, they too can have *all* of the success and happiness that they want. That's exactly why we are so keen to spread the word.

If you look back at where we started out and where we are now, you can clearly see that we've taken this journey ourselves. We're not asking you to do anything that we, or many others, haven't already done before. We've had our challenges and nothing was handed to us on a plate; we simply set our goals, made our life plan and followed it.

Not only have we put our method to the test, we've also got thousands of examples of other people for whom 'The Key' has worked, and you can search for endless success stories on the internet too.

So this is the key that will open a new and exciting future for you. We've given you the key, all you need to do now is take action, by reminding yourself frequently of the key schemas that will make your world a bigger, brighter and better place to be in.

Here's a reminder of your new twelve key schemas:
1.   There is no one reality
2.   Disregard the doubters
3.   Accept responsibility
4.   Anything is possible
5.   Failure only exists when you quit
6.   It's never too late
7.   Plan your life
8.   You are what you eat
9.   Save yourself before you save the world
10.   There are no bad people in the world
11.   You've got to give to receive
12.   You become what you think about

We understand that you may not even want to adopt all twelve schemas, especially if you don't agree with them one hundred percent at this moment in time. Or you may choose to action one each month to entirely transform yourself over the coming year.

The body has limitations, the mind does not. We often focus on what goes on from the neck down, yet we often forget it all starts with the mind. If you're not mentally prepared, then you can never be physically prepared.

It's now up to you. This could be one of the first big choices you make entirely for yourself, by yourself. The first of many. Start now, not tomorrow. You see, once you start, there's a chain reaction, and that allows you to keep going.

As human beings we often feel that so many of our emotions are unique just to us, and we perhaps don't realise that every person suffers from the same problems and that everyone can by default be lazy, as it's the easiest thing to do and requires no effort or energy. So it's a choice not to be lazy, it's a choice not to choose the path of least resistance. But you have got to make the choice to change, you have got to keep practising, keep going, because once you make it through the beginning, that's when it gets fun and you realise you are actually doing this, you are actually changing your life for the better. In the simplest of terms, if you want this, you will find a way to put the effort in; if not, you will find an excuse. There should never be an excuse good enough to deprive you of the amazing life that you totally deserve.

You now need to tap into your self-discipline, which as the term implies comes one hundred percent from you. This will help you adopt the key schemas we have shared, and when you do that you will have more success. Choose to adopt these into your life, and with these new choices you will undoubtedly get new results and transformation, just like we and the many people we have helped have.

We would like to take this opportunity now to wish you the most fantastic life ahead, filled with an abundance of happiness, success and health. We absolutely know that you can become whatever you wish and your future can be amazing if you now follow things through and take steps each day to make it so. We sincerely hope that we will get to meet you personally one day at one of our live events or workshops and hear your success story in person.

We believe in you!

All our love and encouragement,
Nik and Eva Speakman